Clay Supper

Clay Supper

Confessions of a Born Again Christian

by

Dr. Ben M. Carter, Ph.D.

ISBN 978-0615569574

www.drbenmcarter.com

Compiled and edited by Mike's wife,
Salma Carunia Carter

He who tells a story to a fool tells it to a drowsy man;
and at the end he will say, "What is it?"

Ecclesiastics 22:8

And the peace of God, which passeth all
understanding, shall keep your hearts and minds through
Christ Jesus. Finally, brethren, whatsoever things are
true, whatsoever things are honest, whatsoever things
are just, whatsoever things are pure, whatsoever things
are lovely, whatsoever things are of good report; if there
be any virtue, and if there be any praise, think on these
things.

Philippians 4:7-8 (KJV)

CONTENTS

TOADS

And the frogs shall depart from thee, and from thy houses, and from thy servants, and from the people; they shall remain in the river only.

Exodus 8:11

Remember, religion does not so alter the character as to leave something remaining. An ardent and enthusiastic man, when he becomes religious, will still be of the same temperament . . . The timid will be timid still; the person who shuddered at a toad before this conversation, will do the same afterward.

Charles Simeon

I was in Aberdeen Scotland, UK, pursuing my Masters Degree in Theology, when on the morning of October 2, 1985, as I returned from my run on the beach of the North Sea, I met my friend the gray cat. Sometimes he sat in the street. Sometimes he sat on one of the pebbled concrete fence posts that line the riverside of Dartmouth Road. But wherever he sat, he usually "murped" when he recognized me.

It was a little after six, still dark, although behind me the western sky was beginning to harden into blue. Fading like chunks of twinkling imagination, stars flickered in anonymous propriety. The air was dank and I had been running hard and was sweating so my glasses quickly fogged, but I could see the gray cat hunched in the gutter. I was surprised it gave me no greeting. However, approaching him I discovered that his attention was focused upon a little green frog. I, too, stood watching the frog until it escaped down a drain. Then, I greeted the cat who rubbed briefly against my hand before he crept into the brush to follow the path that wound beside the Don River, but the incident I had just witnessed stayed with me. I began to think about frogs in general, and then, about Panama's huge frogs, from when I was in the U.S. Army stationed in Panama, and finally I recalled something that happened later in Puerto Rico.

Now Panama has these horrible toads, as big as croquet balls and lumpy. In the evening, these things came out in unbelievable numbers and lurked around in the grass. They were so evil that they were poisonous and sometimes a dog would attack one and bite it. The poison will do its thing and the dog would die. I don't know if anything could eat them. Perhaps a snake could, but it would have to be a big snake.

Now that would be a picture for our apocalyptically troubled era; a constrictor devouring one of those toads as the toad struggled like Laocoön amid the coils. Suggested title: "Repast." I tried to stay away from toads myself. That I might step on one of the little ogres was a possibility that revolted me. I was afraid that if I did, the creature would curse me before it died. Surely, a curse from a beast that filthy would prove a grievous curse indeed. As the dusk settled and the toads emerged, I would adopt the techniques of jungle movement in which the officers spent so much of their time instructing us. The techniques proved sound for I never stepped upon a toad during the two-and-a half-years that I was stationed at Ft. Kobbe in the Canal Zone.

Such was my perspective in Panama, but the next incident I recalled took place in Puerto Rico. It happened on December 24, 1979. That was my first Christmas as a Christian and I was really up for it! I had been living in the Salvation Army—we called it Sally Ann's—for over a year. In the beginning, I hadn't much liked it, but after I was converted on May 5, 1979, the date of my confession, it got to be kind of fun. All sorts of people came drifting through. The place was a menagerie of sociological oddities. The Hogar Esparañza, where we lived, was in Caparra Terrace, a suburb of San Juan. We lived in Caparra Terrace, a suburb of San Juan, in a place called the Hogar Esparañza, where I met Jay.

Jay was black and said he was from Chicago. I learned when he was in Uncle Sam's Army that most blacks, no matter where they were from, will identify with some northern city as their hometown. On the other hand, if they're a little more hip, they'll claim Seattle or L.A., but they'll not tell you that they're from the South until you get to know them a little better. They do this because they don't want you to think that they've ever shuffled. Sure enough, Jay told me after a few weeks that he had been raised in Mississippi, but he really had lived in Chicago for several years.

In 'Chitown', Jay had met a Puerto Rican girl and they hit if off real well. Jay was hustling on the streets to get his coin, which is a dicey way to affluence, but he liked to gamble. He scored big a couple of times, and eventually he and his lady were able take a major holiday down in Condada, P.R., a beachside, upper class community in the colonial district of Old San Juan.

But once he got down there, Jay got busted and ended in the prison in Bayamon, which is a worse hold than Cook County Jail, if you can imagine that. Anyway, Cupid flew and left Jay doing time, and it was there that Jay met this missionary-type named Bob. Bob ran a prison ministry, and he led Jay to the Lord.

I knew Bob pretty well. He was a good missionary and shepherded a lot of people into the Kingdom. With the cooperation of Captain Victor, who was the jefe at Sally

Ann's, Bob used the Hogar Esparañza as a halfway house for the convicts he really trusted, and Jay was such a convict. For a thug, Jay was a nice guy; his conversion was legitimate and Jesus was doing real work in his life. So, after he had spent a little over a year in the slammer, he was paroled and came to live with us in the Hogar Esparañza. That was in early February 1979. We were baptized together in mid-May.

Jay got out before I did. He wasn't a drunk or anything. He was just a criminal, so he got a job on a construction crew through one of the men at my church. Jay was charismatic, so he went to the Church of the Abundant Life. I was sanctified, so I went to the Wesleyan Church. But we were both believers, so Jay did something that almost never happens: after he left Sally Ann's, he stayed in touch.

He had rented a three room flat above a bar in Caparra Heights and I would go over to see him on Tuesday or Thursday evenings, or on some Saturday mornings. I couldn't go on Wednesday or Friday evenings because of prayer meetings, nor on Monday because of my AA meetings. Some Saturday mornings we worked in the store, but when possible, I'd bounce over and, if Jay were home (which he usually was,) we'd smoke a joint, put on some Christmas tapes, and talk about the Bible, or what God was doing in our lives. On Saturday mornings, Jay would boil some water and make us each a cup of coffee and we would space-out with a little weed and listen to the traffic. Sometimes, Jay, who was quite the raconteur, would tell me stories which I more-or-less pretended to believe. There are few things in the world more pleasant than smoking dope with a friend over a cup of coffee on Saturday morning.

On the morning of Christmas Eve, Captain Victor gave us the day off, so of course I went to see Jay. He made his way to the Church of the Abundant Life. The pastor of that church, Pastor Carl, had a van and Jay was going to borrow it because he had to run some errands for his boss. Jay, too, had the day off but he had agreed to do this as a favor, which meant he was doing it for free. He had some kick-ass smoke, so we got ripped over coffee, and then went to the bus stop because Jay said was too wasted to walk all the way to Carl's church.

On a perfect Caribbean day, mango leaves flickered under a sky that was polished as bright as the throne of God. I was jubilant, elated in my faith. Two thousand years ago the redeemer of the World had been born. Even the weather seemed to be celebrating the event.

Jeremiah must surely be smiling. I could taste the millennium. "Joy to the world, the Lord has come!"
Just before we reached the bus stop, Bob pulled up beside us in his station wagon. He asked us where we were going. We told him, "To Carl's church." Bob was out with his teenage son, Kent. And since he was driving that way anyway, said that we could have a ride if we wanted one, so we hopped in the back. I say, "We hopped," but the last thing in my mind were toads.

Now Jay was engaged to this white girl named Betty and he did eventually marry her. I was the best man—or as Jay said, the second-best man—at the wedding. Betty, from Nebraska, was a nurse and had come to the island to do some short-term missionary service with a couple named Ralph and Jenna.

Her daddy had a ranch. He thought it was a "real fine thing" for his daughter to put her faith into practice like that, especially when so many kids in the heartland were freaking-out. But when he heard that his Betty was planning to marry a black Chicago hustler who had been out of prison for less than a year, he didn't call that "putting her faith into practice." He called that tempting God, and he called anathemas down on everybody. That he was helpless only added to the aesthetic quality of his rage.

The Christian community that we were part of was tight-knit, so everyone knew what was coming down. And as everybody had their own opinion about it, there was opportunity for plenty of controversy and dialogue. As Betty remarked to me once, "We're the most popular couple on the island." Anyway, that's what Bob and Jay talked about on the way over to Carl's church: the engagement. That was fine with me. I was too stoned to want to talk to anybody except myself, but I did enjoy listening to them hassle.

Carl, Jay's pastor, was against the wedding so Jay had asked Pastor Gerard, who was my pastor to perform the ceremony. Bob, who attended church with me, was on Carl's side, but he didn't want to come out and say that he too, was against the wedding. He thought he might still have a little influence with Jay, but he knew he had to tread lightly. So instead, he just kept saying that he thought Carl's opinion ought to count for something, considering Carl was a *gringo* and had married a Puerto Rican girl; but that had nothing to do with it and everyone in the car knew it. The real question was of submission and how they ought to react to Betty's dad. Also, since submission was the question, you could say that Bob, though he was talking to Jay, was also talking to Kent.

Teenagers are rebellious. It's a stage they go through in the West and a necessary step toward independence; but it's a painful stage. Not that Kent was particularly obnoxious. The truth was Jay and I were more obnoxious than Kent. But maybe if Kent hadn't been there, Bob would have felt he could have been less dogmatic.

The circumstances during the preceding weeks had driven Jay deeply into his Bible and he was proof-texting like crazy. I thought his exegesis was good, but he was stoned and the pot tended to make his arguments unnecessarily convoluted. He could see the whole thing so clearly and strove to articulate in all the rich complexity of its elusive detail, his vision of the brotherhood of human beings harbingered in the domestic bliss that God had prepared for him and Betty. They batted Galatians 3:28[1] and Ephesians 6:1[2] and Genesis 26: 34-35[3] back and forth all the way to Carl's church. It was a regular seminar and nobody changed their mind about anything.

By the time we reached the church, I had achieved a prolonged state of cosmic consciousness, which allowed me to comprehend both sides of the issue with complete and absolute clarity; I was in benign agreement with everyone involved. It was all so obvious: possibly yes, possibly no, possibly yes and no, possibly inarticulate, possibly yes and inarticulate, possibly no and inarticulate, possibly yes and no and inarticulate – but after all, who could really say? Having attained such a height of equanimity, I discovered I was able to integrate that comprehension with the motion of the car and the way the light and shadows slid all over the hood and seats. I was everything and everything was me.

Bob parked and as we walked over to Kent's van both he and Jay tried to get the last word in. I floated behind, entranced by the vision of unity revealed behind the manifold of God's created systems. All was one. My foot slipped. I looked down and I staggered forward, and discovered with a lurch in the pit of my groin, that I was back amid the manifold. Squashed on the ground, its life juices still sparkling, was a cousin to one of those ancient Panamanian horrors. I was instantly reminded of Deuteronomy 32:35[4] and that started me thinking about

the wrath of the Lord and Revelation 16: 13-14[5]. All was
not one, and holiness was the witness to that. Like I said
earlier, I was sanctified and belonged to the Wesleyan
Church. That meant I was respectable, since in
Wesleyan parlance, sanctification tends to mean
respectability. The unity of the world had drained through
the hole left by this dead toad. The belief of "all equals
one" gurgled away, leaving sparking multiplicity. God's
holiness blazed up and the world fell apart, casting long
shadows. The equation was gone and in its place was
the Wesleyan synonym "sanctification is respectability." I
shuddered, shook my offended foot and climbed into the
back of the van.

There was another black person with whom I was
baptized, and his name was Brian. He had been in the
Salvation Army with Jay and me, but left shortly after Jay
because Carl let Brian move into a room at the Church of
the Abundant Life.

So, there was Brian waiting for us at the van. He was
charismatic and very handsome but had, since his
conversion, assumed an air of humility, which I found
irritating on occasion because it seemed so genuine. He
was from L.A; I know that's true, because a few months
later he returned to California. I've lost track of Jay, but I
still write to Brian at Christmas. Jay always said that
Brian had it in him to preach, and sure enough, Brian
became a preacher. He was a good friend to Jay, and
like Jay, he worked for Nation Surfacing but he didn't
smoke and didn't know that Jay and I did. I don't think at
that time anyone in the community knew we smoked.
Anyway, I got into the back of the van with my head
buzzing and Brian climbed into the front. Jay started the
motor and eased the van forward. He was a good driver.
As we pulled out, I concentrated on the sound of the
motor—a sound that created a sense of unity—and
struggled to gain control of my scattered thoughts.

I began to remember a sermon that Pastor Gerard had delivered only a few weeks before. It had been about submission. The pastor had said, "The more sanctified one became, the less eccentrically one behaved." The reason for this transformation into conformity, as he explained it, had to do with the new relationship the Christian had to his sense of self. Eccentricity was an assertion of the self. Those who were growing in the Lord were less prone to self-assertiveness and more prone to submit to the standards laid down in scripture and epitomized by the Lord's representatives on earth. In this case, the Lord's representatives were the pastor and elders of the Wesleyan church in Guaynabo. I later ran into the same argument in a letter that Clement of Rome wrote to the church at Corinth toward the end of the first century, and I've often wondered if maybe that's where the pastor got the idea. I had thought about the sermon several times since I heard it, and as it came to mind, I used it as a candle flame to draw the frantic moths of my thoughts.

It began to occur to me that I didn't really much like the idea. Ever since I had been converted, the pastor and all the members in the church had told me that with my conversion, I had been given the mind of Christ. I had also been given a Bible, and the idea was to read the Bible with the mind of Christ, God himself, and through his Holy Spirit, which would lead me into the truth. I mean, the Holy Spirit had inspired the Bible, and the Holy Spirit would tell me what it meant. Now, it seemed to me that what had been given with one hand was being taken away with the other. It looked as though a spirituals hierarchy of pastor and elders was being substituted in place of the Holy Spirit. Of course, there was a place for teachers and preachers, and there was a place for discipline in the church, but weren't these men concerned as they were with respectability and everything? They couldn't even agree on what to do about Jay and Betty!

The question was, "How can I know that I'm saved?" The answer was, "As an evidence of your new status as an adopted child of God, you have been sealed with the Holy Spirit." The second question was, "How can I tell that I'm sealed with the Holy Spirit?" And here things started to get tricky. People sealed with the Holy Spirit didn't habitually commit sin and they were submissive. Now, most of us, being sanctified as we were, didn't think of ourselves as habitually committing sins. We didn't bow down to sticks and stones, habitually kill people, or habitually steal and we didn't vainly repeat prayers or worship the Pope, Mary, or pictures of the saints, or any of that other pagan stuff.

Of course I hadn't done any of that before I was saved, except maybe steal a little and swear, but I'd quit doing both of those after I'd come to know the Lord. Besides there were lots of people in that church who had never done anything wrong since the age of six when they had recognized their need for grace and confessed it to the Lord Jesus. They had gone on in victory helping their mothers around the house, and I had helped my invalid mother around the house, too, come to think about it. But I never was there to help this neighbor kid who died from a methadone overdose when I was twenty-three. I had returned from serving in the U.S. Army as guard at Joint Security Area (DMZ) in Korea. I remembered as he put "Purple Haze" on the family record player and said, "Listen to this" grinning at me with glassy bloodshot eyes.

I guess what I was trying to get at as I sat in the back of that van and Jay told Brian about how important cross-racial marriages were for the fulfillment of God's plan on earth, was that to evidence the presence of the Holy Spirit really meant that one submitted, since none of us sinned habitually anyway. Coupled with this was the concept of abstention. It was important to abstain from things. One shouldn't drink beer, smoke cigars, go to movies, or listen to rowdy music. This abstention was part of our testimony. It was a way of saying, "I'm having more fun than you, and I don't have to do those sorts of things to enjoy myself because I've been changed." But it also helped to define us, helped to remind us that we had been called out, and were no longer of the world. If down the pike, I became unsure of my status, I could always reflect that at one time, I had thrown away all my rock albums and I hadn't seen a movie in x number of donkey's years. It was a kind of baptism; it marked a new beginning.

However, it also meant that we defined ourselves negatively. Our testimony became what we didn't do, not what we did. That was because what we did was (except for going to church on Sunday morning) what everybody else did. We went to school or work, paid our taxes, and obeyed the law. Why, we could even break the law if, when we did, we said we were sorry. I remembered how once a very beautiful high school senior had confessed at evening service to having been part of a group that shoplifted for thrills. She said she had done this for many months, ripping-off stores in the area for thousands of dollars' worth of stuff she didn't need, and much of which she had thrown away. Finally, she had been arrested. No one suggested that she wasn't saved. We thought instead, that hers was a bad testimony, that she wasn't living up to her potential, couldn't dwell together anymore.

It's as if machines distort us somehow because they accentuate some of our abilities. I'm not talking here about comparative weaknesses and strengths. There's a sense in which our failures define us. There are just some things we can't do and that is part of what makes us who we are. But I'm not talking about that. I'm talking about having abilities that are roughly equivalent and having machines that seduce us into giving preference to one ability over another. This is because the machines make the one ability more powerful and the other ability less powerful, because we neglect the other ability and so we are distorted. It's as if I'm given a Bible, and as I read it, Jesus tells me things, so I know those things from his authority. And you have a Bible and Jesus is telling you things, so you speak those things, too, with his authority. Only they're different things from what I'm speaking. So one of us must be deceived and it might be me but if I'm deceived, then whose spirit am I hearing? The more we disagree, the more I wonder, and the uncertainty becomes too terrible and I can't dwell with it anymore. So, I depart and go to the land I have chosen, and hope it's the land of Canaan and not the plain of the Jordan.

I mean look at Jay and Betty. Jay was sincere. He loved Betty and he thought that in her God had given him a good thing, and he wanted to possess that good thing. He wanted to marry her. That's natural enough. But then Betty's father loved her, too, and he had a point. Like Jay, he wanted what was best for her, but from his perspective, it looked like Jay might not be the best. I mean Betty was an R.N. while Jay only had a high school education. Plus Jay had just started his first steady job in years and don't forget, he had a criminal record. I kept thinking Betty's old man was a bigot, that it was the color of Jay's skin that put him off, but that might not be true at all. And then there was the question of submission. I mean, Pastor Gerard said that we in his church ought to submit to him and the elders, who had walked in the Spirit longer and were wiser in the ways of the Lord, and that could be true. My mind changes about things the more I learn that some of those things are spiritual things. Does that mean then that the mind of Christ changes?

But Jay wasn't a member of Pastor Gerard church. He was a member of Pastor Carl's church and Pastor Carl was against the marriage because he thought Jay and Betty should submit to Betty's father. So, Jay and Betty had gone to pastor Gerard and he had agreed to marry them. Was that right? If what pastor Gerard said was true, shouldn't he have insisted that Jay listen to Pastor Carl since he was in Pastor Carl's church, and shouldn't he have refused to marry them? But if what Pastor Gerard said wasn't true, then there was no problem and every man could do what was right in his own eyes. Yet that seemed to me to get at the problem. We were all speaking with the wisdom of men and not with the power of God. That wisdom was like bits of things we found in the streets of the city where we lived, bits of things that we piled in the carts we dragged behind us, and that we were getting further apart from each other all the time. It was ourselves who we were being called away and not the world. It was like the message of Christ was getting to be too respectable, too socialized, too secularized. I mean, there I was, at the door of my first Christmas as a Christian and to celebrate the grand occasion, to make it all a little more intense, I had gotten stoned. I had come to the manger to look at the child who was to die for me and I was stoned. It was just something Jay and I did as a private enjoyment. Yet suddenly it didn't seem like something we did in private anymore. Those wretched and repellant men weren't really isolated at all. They paraded their lives before a myriad of witnesses of whom I was one. In the same way, I was not a private person. I was a member of the body of Christ, the church, bought with a price and surrounded by a cloud of witnesses who had gone before. I was going to have to answer to that child who wasn't a child anymore, but who was in glory, and I was going to have to tell him that I thought I was more important than he was. I was going to show him all the things I had piled in my cart and I was going to say, "Do you see how rich I am? What need do I have of you?" Did I really believe that? Then why didn't I drop that cart and run for shelter to the nearest church? And then I saw that church in her shoddy respectability was just like me. I toked up because I wanted praise, the praise of Jay, the praise of myself, and more than that, I wanted the victory of the Lord and the church was just the same! She had become respectable and had failed to recognize that condition as a judgment upon her from her Lord. And then I realized that Brian was talking to me, telling me to watch for the number of a house, that we were almost there.

CARLA

Many shall be purified, and made white, and tried; but the wicked shall do wickedly: and none of the wicked shall understand; but the wise shall understand

Daniel 12:10

The good has been well defined as that at which all things aim. But it is clear that there is a difference in ends; for the ends are sometimes activities, and sometimes results beyond the mere activities. When there are ends beyond the action, the results are naturally superior to the action

Aristotle

Jay and Betty were married shortly after Christmas a year later. As I said, I was the best man. Brian sent congratulations from California. Betty's parents attended and were very gracious. Jay and Betty had gone to Nebraska to visit them during the summer. Prior to the trip, several of the respectable members of our community had written letters to propitiate the ancestors and reassure them of her life partner. The thrust of these epistles was that Betty was an intelligent and levelheaded woman and sensitive to the leading of the Lord, and that Jay was a man of tremendous potential whose heart had been broken by the Spirit and kindled with love for his Savior. The effect of the letters was to remind Betty's parents of what they already knew, and encourage them in what they hoped was true. The effect of the visit was to confirm the judgment of the letter writers. Her parents could see that Betty was determined on her course. They had to admit that Jay was a very likable man. So they put on the best face they could upon the whole situation. They were all smiles when they arrived. Jay's mother came from Mississippi, bringing Jay's girlfriend and daughter with her.

I knew Jay had a daughter because several months before,
 he had thumb tacked a snapshot of her to his bedroom wall. I may not have recognized her as his daughter had he not pointed out the resemblance to me.   But once he did; I had to admit that she looked pretty much like him. Jay showed me a silver certificate he had been given as change when the subject came up. There is a lot of old money in Puerto Rico, mostly wheat straw pennies, so I was not overly surprised that Jay had been given a silver certificate, but I dutifully praised his good fortune. I realize that Christians should not praise one another's good fortune since we don't believe in luck, but I've never been able to figure out an alternative expression that doesn't sound either pantheistic or else absurdly pious. I just couldn't bring myself to say, "Well, praise the Lord for directing this silver certificate into your hands. Don't we have a mighty God who can do such things for us?" So, I congratulated him on his good fortune and worried a little about Matt. 12: 36-37[6]. As I looked up, Jay pointed to the photo on the wall and asked me, "Do you know who that is?"

"No," I said, "should I?"
"Who does she look like?" Jay pressed.
"A little black girl," I answered tentatively.
"She looks just like me," Jay said. "She looks just like me. She's my daughter."

So I transferred my praise for his dollar to his daughter, and asked about her age and her mother. Jay said that mother and daughter were living happily in Chicago, that his daughter was the sweetest child you could possibly want to meet, and that her mother was a fine woman who he had planned to marry before his life had changed in Puerto Rico. In fact, the completeness of this change had been confirmed to him only the day before, when he was walking past the Libreria Betania, a Christian bookstore dealing in both English and Spanish publications. (This is where I later met my future wife, Salma Carunia, in 1980.) While he was out walking, Jay had begun to wonder if he had really changed as much as he wanted to believe he had. As he was revolving the thought around memories of his old life and his new, he saw a greeting card in the window of the store. The card was a photograph of the sun hung low over the sea. The basic color of the card was blue, but the blue was vibrant with golden rays bursting across the waves from between cumulo-stratus clouds massed beyond the horizon. Over these rays were printed the words: "Behold, I make all things new. Rev. 21:5[7]." It was, Jay observed, as if God has spoken to him. He truly was a new creature. His doubts scattered and his heart leaped like the waves. Men had issued no warrants against him. Before God, his past was covered by Christ's blood; and that past included mother and daughter.

At evening service on the Sunday before the wedding, I met the follies for whom Jay had been forgiven. They stood beside Jay and Betty and sang carols. I sat in the pew in front of them. Jay's girlfriend was named Carla and she was a very charming woman. I didn't realize at first what her relationship to Jay was and mistook her for his sister, but when I met the daughter, I remembered the photo. I looked from the little girl straight at Betty, but Betty seemed as serene as the child herself.

A week or so before, Jay had moved into a larger apartment at the top of a modern complex that towered among the hills on the outskirts of the city. His mother, his girlfriend, and his daughter were staying there with him until after the wedding. The wedding was to be performed on Saturday morning. Jay and Betty were to leave Saturday afternoon for a weeklong cruise. Mother, girlfriend, and daughter were to depart the next morning. Before the wedding, we would celebrate Christmas.

Ralph and Jenna had two daughters, Daisy, who was fifteen, and Joan, who was ten. Joan was retarded. I arrived early on Christmas morning, bringing a chocolate Santa Claus for Joan. Ralph and Jenna presented me with Halley's Handbook of the Bible. I wasn't too much into commentaries at the time. I didn't want men to tell me what the Bible meant; I wanted the Holy Spirit to do the job himself. In retrospect, this mind-set strikes me oddly for I have since discovered that those who write the commentaries might themselves be guided by the Holy Spirit. But at the time, I was still innocent and thought that Jesus Christ as I understood him to be was Jesus Christ as he is. I did not yet realize that I was dealing with a tradition founded in an event that had occurred some two thousand years ago.

Jay and Betty arrived shortly after I did and the morning was spent in laughter and fellowship. Christians often describe themselves as a family. I think that the metaphor is a little overworked since it would be very inappropriate for church members to become as intimate with one another as the term family implies. But on that particular day such niceties of distinction, had they occurred to me, would have seemed out of place. There really was a sense in which, at least for a while, those in that room became as a family.

As noon approached Jenna, Daisy and Betty began to set the tables. There were two tables; a larger one where we would sit and which the women piled with good things to eat, and a smaller one where no one sat and which served to catch the overflow of dishes that could not be squeezed onto the larger table. The kitchen became the horn of Amalthaea and gave forth lavishly. When I asked her, Jenna told me that her Christmas dinners were events she engineered months in advance. The ministry in which she and the Ralph were engaged left them with little leisure, so it was not difficult for me to believe her as I surveyed the result. After a couple of hours, Jay excused himself and went to pick up Carla but Betty and I remained amid the feast. I was determined to eat as much as I could. One of the advantages of being a single man in an evangelical church is that one discovers who the really good cooks are.

I was still making room for another bite when I heard Jay's VW pull into the driveway. A minute later, Jay popped through the back door and said that we had better get moving if we wanted to go to the beach. Daisy demurred. Betty and I followed Jay out to the car where he had left Carla waiting. I climbed into the back and Jay asked Carla, who was sitting in the front, if she would mind getting into the back with me. She complied and Betty took her place in the front. Jay strapped himself in behind the wheel and we were off. The sky was brilliant that Christmas afternoon and it was very hot.

I don't know what the nights were like in Jay's apartment when that strange little family found itself alone, but as we drove to the beach I began to sense that Carla, though confronted with what was practically a fait accompli, had not accepted the situation as passively as I had at first believed. I got the impression that she and Jay had done some fast hard talking on the way back from his apartment. Even with the windows down, the car seemed a trifle close. It was obvious that in the child, Carla had a trump card she could play if she chose. But even if she could contrive to ruin the wedding and perhaps destroy the marriage before it got fairly off the ground (and I suspected that she was a woman capable of doing at least that), I couldn't see how she would gain much from it except revenge. Her revenge could be devastating, so she had a lot of potential power. But if she had come only to destroy, I couldn't see why she delayed. She seemed more like she wanted something. But perhaps she didn't realize how much power she had. No one was trembling before her. She probably had no inkling how strenuous the objections of Betty's father had been, how she could, at a minimum if she introduced him to the child, wreck the fragile bridges that the letters and the visit had built and split that little Nebraska family wide open, maybe for the decades. I began to wonder if anyone besides Betty and me knew who she was. And then I began to appreciate how ruthless Jay could be. Here, it seemed to me, was the essence of ruthlessness, not grim in the course it pursued, but blasé. Jay's nonchalance was marvelous to behold. As far as he was concerned, the past was dead even if its children lived on. And on this point, Betty was of one mind with him. Her confidence in him was boundless, almost reckless. And I began to see that Jay's easy assurance was firmly anchored in his confidence. He knew his woman. I was to discover that he knew them both. He could see all the cards and he was certain that he was going to win.

When we got to the beach Jay and Betty wandered off leaving Carla and me to entertain ourselves as best we could. We had two points of contact with which to begin our acquaintance. One was Jay and one was the beach. We chose the safer route and began to wander down the sand among the merrymakers who thronged Condado in gregarious luxury. The communist takeover of Cuba was a blessing for Puerto Rico. The flow of U.S. dollars, which had been transforming Havana into a sybaritic paradise, was rechanneled to Puerto Rico, awakening that drowsy Catholic island to this bustling post-Protestant century. Everywhere we looked the post-Protestants were burning their shoulders and sucking rum, fruit juice, and melted ice through colorful straws. Their efforts to have a good time were fueled by the knowledge of how much their vacation down here was costing them. Buttocks of divers' weights and measures were molded into patterned bikinis of various hues. I saw a man stretched mournfully in a lawn chair, a tropical drink gripped in his right hand and the tassel of a red Santa's hat he wore running like candle wax down the back of his head. His was the only lawn chair on the beach. He was graying at the temples and wearing maroon trunks and looked so absurdly miserable that I nudged Carla and nodded in his direction. She smiled a little. I wanted to proclaim the Word to that milling horde of unbelievers, to tell them what the season was really all about, to cry to the man in the Santa's hat that he was a being of tremendous significance. I wanted to say how God had acted in history because of that significance, and that his response to that cosmic deed would determine his status in eternity forever. But he didn't look like he would be much interested, and besides, having gotten Carla to smile, I wanted to find out what I could about her and the life she and Jay had before.

I won't tell you that she described her current circumstances in any great detail. She had a nice flat. She enjoyed entertaining. She was an inspector for food manufacturing company in their quality control department. She briefly recounted her duties and assured me (in case I had any doubts about the matter) that the company went to great lengths to guarantee excellence in their product. She herself did not care much for their stuff but she could recognize, even if she could not appreciate, their achievement. Indeed, it was her job to keep them up to scratch. She was very proud of that. Jay's mother had notified her that Jay was to marry, and she had arranged to accompany Jay's mother to San Juan. She was guarded when I tried to learn her reasons for coming and she would say nothing of the Jay she knew. She was not there to praise or blame him, at least to me. Our conversation was in a room too small to support its need for oxygen and Carla would not help me open the door to free it. Thwarted, the conversation grew weary and gasping lay down to die. Then Jay and Betty came walking up.

I had not yet been to his new apartment so, instead of returning to Ralph and Jenna, Jay drove us across town to see it. He lived on the eighteenth floor of a recently completed high-rise. The kitchen was to our left as we entered. The dining area was separated from the kitchen by a counter, and was itself, part of the living room. At the far end of the room, I could see sliding glass doors, which opened to a balcony. Midway down the left wall of the living room was a door, which opened into the bedroom. Except for a double bed in there, and the dining table and chairs in the dining area, the flat, though carpeted, was completely unfurnished. There was a radio on the dining table and near the table was a magazine rack in which I saw a couple of copies of *Ebony*. I recognized the rack from Jay's other apartment. As Jay took me through the rooms, he told me how he and Betty were planning to decorate. Carla joined Jay's mother and daughter who were already there, but Betty went along with us and supplemented Jay's remarks with observations of her own.
When we came back into the living room, Jay asked his mother how her day had gone and if the child had behaved. Without any warning at all, Carla, as though she was inquiring about the weather, asked, "What do you think is going to happen to your daughter?"

"I guess what's been happening to her since I've been gone," Jay responded without a bobble. Jay's mother was impassive. It was as though she had not heard. Betty's smile became slightly fixed. I forgot I was standing there. I couldn't have looked away from those four people if I had remembered to try.

"I've been raising her is what," Carla answered him. Her voice had a slight edge to it. Then the edge was gone and she went on matter-of-factly, "I thought you'd be coming back."

There was an almost imperceptible pause before Jay responded, "Well, things have worked out pretty well for me down here. You can see how things have changed. I guess you've lost me."

This was not dismissal, this was absolution. As I said, I don't know what they talked about at night. I've tried to imagine it but I suspect that imagination, even at it's most fecund, images the extant but poorly. Even at its most fantastic, fiction is a pale shadow of truth, if only because God is smarter and more creative than we are. And I don't know for sure what was going on then but I think they had forgotten about me as I had forgotten about myself. This scene, I thought, was being performed for Betty's benefit. If Carla was to present her case, her appeal would begin now and would be to Betty. She had evidently decided that further adjuration before Jay was useless. She would solicit Betty's sympathies. She would entreat her woman-to-woman, and the foundation of her appeal would be the child. She was facing Jay but I expected her to turn toward Betty. However, Jay was pressing his suit as well and, really, the momentum was with him. It's quite possible that Betty, like me, had known about the child before Carla came, but had attached little significance to some abstract toddler in far off Chicago. How was she to know that flesh and blood would confront her on the eve of her marriage? And that marriage, which had demanded so much of her emotional stamina, which had been over a year in the making, and which had been debated and blessed by our spiritual leaders, was to take place in just a few days. Even her father had finally consented and had thrown his weight behind the affair, traveling two thousand miles to attend. Now the ethics of all this could have been called into question, especially when actually met the child, but there just wasn't the time, money, or energy to discuss it anymore. Besides, I wasn't sure that anybody outside of this room really knew what was going on. No, the marriage was like a Jagannath crashing through the streets of Calcutta and I didn't think a child in its path was going to be able to stop. But Carla did not turn to Betty, and she made no further reference to the child at all. Instead, still staring at Jay, she said, "You're going to marry a white woman." She sounded incredulous, exasperated.

Jay turned to me and said, "Well, this is the place. It might not look like much now, but there's a lot we can do with it. Now let's go and get some more of Jenna's food, and then I'll take you home." He took Betty by her arm and with this gesture began to usher Betty and me out. As I turned to go, Carla's face was nothing but two eyes, a nose, and a closed mouth. Anything that lived in there had dropped like a sail behind the dome of the sea, and there was nothing left but vacant sky and smooth deep water. On the way back to Ralph and Jenna, Jay talked about plans he had for starting his own company. He figured he could do as good a job as his boss and didn't see why he should work for him longer than he had to. Of course, something like that would take a few years to work out, but it was definitely worth pursuing. What had happened in the room was as though it had never been, nor did I ever hear him refer to it again.

On Thursday evening, we had the wedding rehearsal. Everything went fine until Betty burst into tears as she was coming down the aisle with her father. Jay was there in a second and took her to the back of the church, where he talked with her earnestly for a few minutes. Betty's father sat in a pew. The rest of us remained standing where we were. Then Jay led Betty back to her father and we went through the rest of the mock ceremony.

Jenna was all sympathy for Betty and dismissed the incident as a case of pre-wedding jitters. I suppose that in a way, she was right.

Late Friday afternoon, Jay came by my room on Central Avenue and drove me down to Santurce to pick up my tux. I had not known for sure when he was coming and had waited for several hours, becoming depressed. At one point, I had tried to alleviate my despondency by reading Christ's Sermon on the Mount, but the now familiar words seemed tedious and distant. It was as though I was standing at the back of the crowd and wasn't catching everything. In the end, I put the Bible aside and read several rather dreary selections from a collection of horror short stories I had discovered at the Salvation Army store. It was with some relief that I put the book aside when Jay knocked on my door. Jay was, as you might expect, excited. Between work and the wedding, he had been on a dead run all day. He gave me a rambling account of the day's activities as he drove. When we got to the tuxedo rental shop, Jay asked the proprietor if he could have my suit ready when we came for Jay's suit in the morning. I thought it was awfully short notice, but the man assured us as he took my measurements that it would be no problem. Jay told me as we got back in his VW that he would come by early to get me.
He arrived shortly before eight-thirty. The morning was radiant, but as the day wore on the sky grew hazy and by late afternoon had become overcast. We swung by the tuxedo rental shop. The suits were ready, so we signed for them and hung them carefully in the back seat of the car. Then Jay drove by the church to see how the preparations for the reception were going. The reception was to be held in a long hall beneath the sanctuary. When we got there, it was being decorated by three women, one of whom told Jay that her husband had gone to get the cake. Jay entered the sanctuary and looked

around. Then we climbed back into his VW and left. As we were driving away, Mick Jagger was on the radio complaining to someone that he was so hot for her and she was so cold, we saw Pastor Gerard coming toward us in his Lincoln sedan. He rolled down his window and waved us over. Jay turned the knob on the radio and Mick Jagger became a querulous whisper.

"I just wanted to touch bases with you," Pastor Gerard said, "I'm on my way to the house but I should be back to church a little after eleven. Is everything okay on your end?"
"Yeah." Jay nodded. "We're heading to my place now to dress. They and my mother are there. I should have everyone over to the church before eleven-thirty. I took Betty by Jenna's already. I guess they're getting her ready now."

Pastor Gerard registered this intelligence with a nod and a wave. Jay turned the radio back up as we drove off. I hung my arm out the window and pressed my hand against the door. The metal was hot from the sun. Mick Jagger's complaints filled the car like a bull roar. I tapped my foot to the frantic music. The song fit my mood exactly. I wanted to smash something brittle.

When we reached Jay's apartment, I went to his bedroom and changed quickly into my tux. Jay's mother, his daughter, and Carla were already dressed. They were standing in the living room when we came in. I could hardly look at them.

On our way downtown yesterday evening, Jay and I had agreed that it might be fun if we had a little rum before the ceremony. When I had come into the apartment, I had seen a couple of unopened quarts on the kitchen counter along with two large bags of potato chips. I supposed he was planning on a private reception after the public one at the church. When I came out of the bedroom wearing my tux, I walked over to the counter and opened one of the bottles. I took a quick swig and could tell by the way my stomach lurched that I was out of practice. I found two six packs of Coke in the refrigerator and a bowl of ice cubes in the freezer. I took a tumbler from the cupboard above the sink and poured a healthy slug of rum into it. Then I added two cubes of ice and a little Coke. The pop of the can sounded so loud when I opened it that I glanced up from the counter and saw that the two women were watching me, so I asked them if I could make them a drink. Jay's mother said nothing, but Carla shook her head shortly and said, "No."

Walking past them with my drink, I stepped out on the balcony. I was very upset. When I became a Christian, I quit drinking and had drunk nothing for seventeen months. Then in October, I had gone out one Sunday evening after church with a fellow named Big Eric, and he and I had split a fifth of Jack Daniels between us. Then a couple of weeks ago, I had gotten drunk at a company Christmas party, and once I had gotten drunk on a Sunday afternoon. I did not want to start drinking again, but I was feeling completely irresponsible. I took a long pull from the tumbler, then another. Then I leaned on the balustrade and looked down at some African tulip trees in full bloom across the parking lot. They were big as chestnuts, only instead of white flowers; they were speckled with orange ones. I was dressed in a tux and stood on a balcony with a glass half empty in my hand. My face was pensive. In the distance were hazy Caribbean mountains, the Cordia Central that begins in the Oriente province of Cuba, reaches its highest points in Hispanola, and climaxes in the waterfalls of El Unque in the Luquillo National Forest thirty miles east of San Juan. I must have looked as elegant as a manikin in an ad, but I could feel myself collapsing into chaos.

I must try to explain to you what bothered me, why I felt so volatile, what there was about Jay's marriage, and Jay's daughter and Carla, and my own resumption of those drinking patterns that had cost me the third decade of my life, which for me at least had assumed cosmological significance. Like Jay, when he had been walking past the bookstore some months back, I too, had been asking myself if I had really changed as much as I wanted to believe I had. My first year as a Christian had been a very good time for me, but during the last few months, doubts and desires that I thought had been put to rest forever had reawakened and would not stay rebuked. Was I really expected to believe that there were opossums and koalas on the ark? And if not, had others besides Noah survived the Flood? Yet, God had made a covenant with Noah and through Noah with all men. If others besides Noah survived (and so far as I knew, men had been hunting mastodons in North America some fifty thousand years ago), then what became of that covenant? And speaking of hunting, did I really believe that there had been a time on this earth when there was no death or disease? Or, more to the point, could I believe that? Again, if God loved us and wanted us to walk in victory, and if Satan was defeated, why couldn't I submit and walk in that victory all the time? I did not deny that my life had changed, but I did not understand my failures. To say that all my failures were mine while all my victories belonged to Jesus only increased my confusion. If Jesus was winning victories for me, why was he still allowing failure in those areas of my life where I so desperately coveted victory? Besides, I wanted assurance that I was being recreated by the Holy Spirit rather than recreating myself by willfully conforming my actions to a particularly efficacious system of symbols. And what prevented me from crying to those people on the beach that they were going to fry in Hell forever if they didn't repent? If somebody was going to start machine-gunning them, and I knew it, I would sure start yelling and let them think what they would. But it wasn't

just a question of frantically yelling. I couldn't even walk up to some joker in a Santa Claus hat and say, "Hey, Jack, do you know you're significant?" I didn't think he would take me seriously. He might even start yelling.

And this was where Jay's marriage came in. Now, I have to be very careful here. I've told you everything about the circumstances leading up to the marriage, everything at least that I knew and that seemed significant to me. The events might strike you differently than they struck me. But let me tell you how I felt.
In the first place, I didn't feel particularly sorry for Jay's daughter. Many kids live in one-parent homes and, while that's a shame, at least Carla was employed and seemed on the surface of things to be a good mother. The little girl was well behaved and showed no signs of physical abuse. I couldn't say I felt particularly sorry for Carla. She seemed like a tough enough lady and certainly hadn't played her scenes to elicit any sympathy from me. I didn't know why she had come down for the wedding. Maybe she was trying to put something right between her and Jay. Maybe she had come down ready to spit bullets, but had lost her nerve when she got on Jay's turf. What had happened in Jay's apartment a few days before seemed, the more I reflected, to have been inexplicable. If it had been directed at Betty, what did it mean? Yet, she had not addressed Betty in the end as I had expected. To the last, she had addressed herself to Jay and it was certain that Jay wasn't awed by her. But I was awed by Jay. He seemed so completely untroubled by the sorts of things that badgered me, or, if he was troubled, his doubts were put to rest quickly. To see a card in a shop window was all he needed. Was that faith or megalomania? Was there a standard beyond the standard of success that one could use to distinguish between the two? And did

not the raising of Lazarus and parable of the fool who built bigger barns, Luke 12:13-21[8], put the quietus on mere success as a standard for spirituality? I mean, the hand of the Lord was with Dan and he prospered in all he did, but the hand of the Lord was with John the Baptist too, and he got stuck with locusts and wild honey.

I finished the rest of my drink. Already the alcohol was doing its thing and I was feeling much calmer. If there was distress in prayer, there was repose to be found in the bottle. This, at least, was for sure: the African tulip trees were beautiful, and beauty witnesses to God even if it only witnesses to his holy wrath.

MEOW MAN

And thou shalt bestow that money for whatsoever thy soul lusteth after, for oxen, or for sheep, or for wine, or for strong drink, or whatsoever thy soul desireth; and thou shalt eat there before the Lord thy God, and thou shalt rejoice, thou, and thine house-

Deuteronomy 14:26

"Are you never tempted?" asked Faith, half-scornfully; "and yet I doubt not you were well baptised!"
"True," said Lois, sadly; "I often do very wrong, but, perhaps, I might have done worse, if the holy form had not been observed."

Elizabeth Gaskell, *Lois the Witch*

I smoked my first marijuana cigarette when I was seventeen. The young neighbor boy, who lived down the street, gave it to me one damp and windy November night. As I mentioned before, he died of a methadone overdose a few years after he got out of the Navy. Talk about a stereotype! On that November night, I knew only three other people who did drugs, but by the time I turned twenty almost everyone had become a dope smoking fiend. It was like a twisted Pentecost as the strobes flashed, the albums blared, and the converts multiplied. We drifted from suburbia into the city, took over entire municipal districts, got ripped and radical, and rapped about our insights.

Years later, after I had become a Christian, I read Kant's Critique of Pure Reason, and recognized the mechanism by which these insights came. Truth is relative to perception; it exists in tension between the objective and subjective.

The processes of comprehension are chemical; modify the chemistry and you modify the perception and comprehension. Thus, to alter the chemical basis of the subjective, transforms the objective by reshaping our apprehension of it. Presto: insight.

As Huxley points out in <u>Heaven and Hell</u>, asceticism, because it too, alters the body's homeostatic state, produces a similar visionary disposition. The yogi and the doper are into the same kind of thing, a private vice, which in the case of the yogi, is a little more refined. The interest in Hinduism, which developed within the drug scene, seems a natural enough phenomenon when I observe it at two decades distance. The oneness of all things is a perception that has its roots in the unity of the self, and I suspect that could be demonstrated in the laboratory. I mean, we're talking about intoxication here—the breakdown of categories, the blurring of distinctions, higher and higher levels of generalization building to an absolute whole.

Interestingly enough the word translated as witchcraft (KJV) or sorcery (RSV) in Galatians 5:20 is φαρμακεία from which we get our word <u>pharmacy</u>. As late as the seventeenth century, the practice of φαρμακεία by Christians was regarded as an unforgivable sin from Hebrews 6:4-6[9] and I John 5:16[10]. God incarnate had called it blasphemy of the Holy Spirit (Matthew 12:31-32[11]), or so they thought back then.

Today, we consider all that nonsense. Indeed, Ryrie's footnote to the Matthew passage assures us that it is not currently possible to blaspheme the Holy Spirit, but I remain skeptical. It strikes me that there is still at least one sin for which forgiveness, if not actually refused, is at least reserved.

I have noticed that if something goes amiss and there is a drunk anywhere in the area, the drunk will be blamed.

In part, this is because drunks, like children, are prone to get into things; and in part, it is because drunks are obnoxious. But I think it is also because we live in a society that puts a high priority on respectability and efficiency, and the drunk, being what he is, can be neither. Therefore, no matter what, the drunk is wrong.

This truth has been born home to me on many occasions and I have found that, as a truth, it is no respecter of persons. Contempt for those who habitually abuse alcohol is common among those who habitually abuse other drugs, and it is even nurtured by drunks themselves. I don't think this can be dismissed as mere hypocrisy. It seems instead that it indicates the all-pervasiveness of cultural conditioning. I recall, for example, what occurred one August night in 1977.

I was living on Warren Street in Milwaukee, Wisconsin, about a block off Brady, which is the heart of the eastside. It happened only a week or so before I had run into an old friend named Brad. I had known Brad between 1970 and 1972 when he lived on Neuhall Street. He had worked as a factory electrician for one of the auto manufacturers, making plenty of money—an excellent source for drugs—so, I was pleased that he was still in town. However, his circumstances had radically changed, about a hundred and forty-six degrees, since I had gone into the Army. Brad had lost his job, divorced his wife, and moved in with a chick named Helen, who tended bar to keep them clothed and housed. She was working at Murphy's Landing at the time. She was still pretty good looking, but she drank heavily and so did Brad. On this particular night, Brad and I went to the Speed Queen to pick up some ribs, then swung by Murphy's Landing, which was closing, to pick up Helen and a six pack of Old Style to wash down the grease. The bar had closed and Helen was waiting for us with the beer. She climbed into the Rambler, kissed Brad, and started cussing at some clown, who an hour or so before had gotten nasty after his eighth or ninth double. In the end, she had to have him thrown out. "I don't know why people act like that," she finished.

"Well, gee Helen," I said artlessly, "the guy was drunk." Brad turned and snapped, "So, he was drunk? What's that? A license to act like an asshole?"

Well, there it was. I mean in one sense, we use drunkenness in just that way. Somebody was a pig the night before, and then apologizes, saying that he wasn't himself; he was drunk, and we accept his apology on those grounds. Sometimes we will make excuses for a drunk, telling ourselves that we must try to understand that, after all, the person was drunk, whether the person apologizes or not. But on the other hand, Brad was right. We don't recognize drunkenness, especially habitual drunkenness, as an excuse for anything. Instead, we condemn it as a great evil, and that's what Brad was saying. I was immediately silenced, recognizing in Brad's question, a judgment that was closer to the truth than my attempt to minimize Helen's cause for grievance, and I wasn't the only one silenced.

The car became quiet. The three of us, after all, were living pretty boozy lives. But the position, accepted as an absolute, can be very destructive. Even the Hebrew law was coupled with the prophetic admonition to mercy (Micah 6:8[12]), which brings me to the subject of Meow Man.

In the Salvation Army there were those who stayed and those who didn't. Naturally, those who didn't stay had no regular jobs, but those who did stay were assigned occupations in the spirit of II Thessalonians 3:10[13], a passage to which idlers were unhesitatingly referred. For example, there was Jed. Jed worked on the rag machine baling clothes, which had been donated and could not be sold. Every day we would bring in at least one truckload of <u>ropas</u>. Now, I'm talking about fresh, ready-to-wear garments here. Many were on hangers and still boasted laundry tags. Donations are not garbage. Sally won't accept shoddy goods. Of course, her clientele are not sufficiently numerous to purchase a truckload or more of clothes a day. This is the era of the well-dressed poor. Even in Puerto Rico, which survives on imports, and where, as the saying goes, you have to pay for the trip. New clothes of fine quality are fairly inexpensive. There just isn't a booming market for second hand ropas as should be evident from the steady and heavy donations. People regularly clean out their closets. So apparel stacked up on the shelves in the back and rotted, creating an ecosystem of fabric, cockroaches, mice, and mildew. This is where Jed came in. Every morning we would pile enough clothes beside Jed's baling machine to keep him busy for the rest of the day. Once a week, usually on Friday, we would run a truckload of the baled clothes over to a scrap metal merchant who had contracted to buy them. But even with Jed's ceaseless labor, we fell back steadily before the advancing walls of polyester.

Brian, when he was there, was put to work in the book section. We were given almost as many books and magazines as we were given clothes. We had plenty to read and plenty to wear. These books covered the gambit from Spinoza's <u>Ethics</u>, to manuals on magic. We were given <u>The Watchtower</u>, <u>National Geographic</u>, and <u>Childcraft,</u> and Captain Victor tried to peddle them all. Such indiscriminant enterprise provoked criticism. After he was converted, Brian would destroy texts on the occult before they reached the shelves, and once, Bob the missionary stormed in and confiscated all Captain Victor's Ouija boards and burned them, refusing to give the captain a penny for them. It didn't make much difference though. There was plenty more where they'd come from, far more than we could handle. In the back, Book Mountain grew—decayed, eroded, and crumbled across the floor as it nurtured vermin.

Shoes were even harder to sell than books, but there was a fellow who was employed in sorting the most marketable zapatos, which he then displayed to their best advantage along a shadowy section of the wall in the rear near the books. The rest were boxed and stored, and eventually trucked to the dump on those Saturday mornings when we went in to the store to work.

Phonograph records didn't sell at all, but we had a wide selection at the front of the store: polka bands, Mozart, harp soloists, Herman and the Hermits. In the back, toiled Danilo, who repaired electric appliances. He who had been born in the Dominican Republic, and had travelled all over the South Pacific with the Merchant Marines. Martin always went out on the trucks with Danilo, the driver, and I usually went out with Stan after I had been there a few months and gotten a little seniority; and so it went. Those who stayed were given something to do.

But not everyone worked at the Santurce store. There were jobs to be done back in the Hogar Esparañza. Laundries Man was in charge there. He cooked, did the laundry, and wandered around with a broom. He needed an assistant, but his assistants usually asked for other jobs after a fairly short time because Laundries Man could be difficult. Ned, a lean long-limbed American, who in his early forties was learning to mystify himself with daydreams, took Jose's place. Ned was followed by Mexico who was volatile. Dan, another American, who was drifting north out of the Caribbean, relieved Mexico, but was himself replaced in a week or so by Mani, and so it went. The slot was a revolving door until Meow Man filled it. I have no idea how he and Laundries Man were able to get along. You would have thought that two poisons would have produced poison but sometimes they produce salt, and I guess that is what happened in this case.

Meow Man was a psychopath; a cesspool of latent violence, a low-rent dude. That's how he got the name Meow Man. It happened this way; the warehouse at the back of the store was like a Chinese puzzle of habiliments, furniture, appliances, dismal toys, no one could remember exactly what. Whole sections had become almost impenetrable and these naturally attracted nesting animals.

I don't recollect who found the kittens, but I know that it was after Captain Victor had summoned the animal control people to clear out all the dogs. The density of the cat population in the neighborhood began to shift toward the warehouse, and one day, the kittens were discovered. Their eyes weren't even open, which was just as well, given the heaps of dust in that part of the vast shed made of wood, cinder blocks, and corrugated tin alloy that served as our stockroom. Word got around, and we the subjugated went to have a look, but nobody told the captain anything because we as the subjugated could still remember the wails of the terrified dogs as they were roped and dragged away. We kept the secret of our new mascots nervously to ourselves.

Then a few days later, as we were preparing to leave the store at the end of the afternoon, it was discovered that the kittens had been strangled. We were outraged as we carried their tiny bodies to the garbage. But everyone felt a little creeped-out, too. What kind of person would strangle a nest of kittens and then leave them to be discovered by those who had watched over them so anxiously? Worse, we all suspected it was one of us. Who else knew the cats were there? The unpleasant mystery was very much on our minds as we took our seats in the blue and white Chevy van, which was Sally Ann's family car. Meow Man was a recent arrival who said little and did less. As we speculated somberly among ourselves, Meow Man began to mew softly. After he had attracted our attention, he leered and chuckled, "Gatitos morta." He continued to chuckle even after everyone had looked away, and occasionally for the next day or two, he would mew so we began to call him Meow Man. In less than a fortnight, he went to work for Laundries Man and he stayed.

Meow Man was clean-shaven with steel-gray hair, which he combed back and kept short. Very light on his feet, he was powerfully built with broad shoulders, a barrel chest, and a nascent paunch. I do not remember that he ever smiled. Laundries Man was a few years younger, though his black hair, which was wavy, and which he brushed back in a kind of bushy crew cut was streaked with gray. Like Meow Man, he was clean-shaven and morose, but in contrast to Meow Man, he was short, wiry, and walked with a limp. These two splashed rice on our trays, washed our silverware, and loomed and receded around the kitchen like the twin halves of the moon. They waxed and waned mellifluently until the evening when Nacio came in drunk. But by that time, Meow Man had been orbiting with Laundries Man for several months.

Nacio must have been in his mid-twenties. He had enrolled in the program only a few days before. I say "enrolled in the program" because Nacio said he had a drinking problem and had come to Sally's to try to kick it. He was young for that, but it does happen. I was there after all, and I wasn't much older, and Dan, too, was young, a little younger than I was. But Nacio was younger than his years. He acted like a kid and was punkie. He should have been kept in for a month, but that rule wasn't always strictly enforced. For example, I had been allowed to go out my first weekend after signing up in December and did not have to do my thirty days until I came in drunk in early January. Dan, on the other hand, began his thirty days immediately. Anyway, Nacio was allowed out, and shortly before the evening meal, he came in, weaving and sore at a couple of the men. There was something of a row, not much, you know, just some angry words; but Adam, who was in charge at the time, and himself a beneficiary of the program, was called to calm Nacio down. Now this sort of thing happened frequently. SOP was to send the offender to bed, or if he was too rowdy, to chuck him outside and let him sleep it off in the street, then next morning to have a chat with him privately and restrict him for thirty days. It isn't called the Salvation Army for nothing. Normally, a person was given two chances, or maybe three, before he was thrown out for good. Nacio wasn't going to be able to deny that he had been drinking, and he didn't try, but he did deny that he was drunk. In answer to Adam's question he responded, "Si, si, dos cervazas pero nada mas." Everything was going according to script. Of course, Adam didn't believe that red-eyed, furry-tongued lie for a minute, but he knew the game. He'd played it himself from the other side. How much Nacio drank was unimportant. What mattered, and they'd talk over it tomorrow in Adam's office, was that Nacio had drunk punto. A bottle of beer was as good as a quart of rum. Adam had the admission, and that was what he wanted. It was time for chow, so Adam told Nacio to go on in and eat, and then clean up and crash. Nacio said, "Gracias" and went into the dining hall. So far, it looked like the hand was being played out in the normal way, but there were two jokers in the pack. The first was that, in spite of appearances, Adam was furious. He disliked Nacio because Nacio was punkie and he had pegged him as a Jonah on this gospel ship. The second was Meow Man.

I was late for chow that day, so I was only about halfway done when Nacio carried his tray over to the sink where Meow Man was doing the dishes, scraped his scraps into the garbage, and dropped the tray in the water. I was facing in that direction, so I saw the whole thing. There was a knife-rack near the sink, and in one of the slots of this knife-rack was an ice pick. I suppose it must have been used for something, but I don't know what. Chopped ice was not a common commodity among us. But the kitchen was better equipped than it needed to be, and the ice pick, used or not, was handy. Meow Man had it before the soap bubbles that had splashed the front of his shirt popped and he went after Nacio like Joab went after Absalom. Nacio thrust the garbage can between Meow Man and himself and started yelling, "Que pasa..? Que pasa..?" But Meow Man kept coming, stabbing with the ice pick, and ramming him with the garbage can that Nacio himself had seized for protection. The can, as they wrestled around it, made a terrible clatter. Now all this happened in far less time than it takes to read it, and it was completely unexpected. I mean, I sat there thinking, "These guys are acting like a couple of brats. What a tantrum over a little water." Then a couple of other guys jumped up and rushed the two combatants. One of them grabbed Meow Man and one of them grabbed Nacio, and Nacio and Meow Man froze. As soon as everything was over, the whole place broke into a hubbub.

Adam was raging. He told me later that he would have called the cops to arrest Nacio if Meow Man hadn't been involved. Adam was pleased with the job that Laundries Man and Meow Man were doing and he was glad that, for once, somebody had been able to stay with Laundries Man for longer than a few weeks. So he didn't want to put the squeeze on Meow Man, but as far as Adam was concerned, Nacio should have been thrown in the can for splashing that soap. Adam was an American and had spent some time in Bayamon Prison for armed robbery.

He had come to know the Lord through Bob. His favorite verses were Philippians 4:8-9[14] and he was convinced that Nacio was pure infectious trouble.

As it was, Adam and several of the other men threw a bewildered and unresisting Nacio into the street along with the few items he had accumulated during his brief sojourn among us. Then the victorious party marched back inside and locked the rejas behind them. Nacio stood dazed in the street for a few seconds, looking from the Hogar Esperañza, to his things, and back again to the Hogar. Then he collected his scant belongings and walked off toward the De Diego. I never saw him again. Meow Man was back at the dishes when I finished my meal. I was careful not to splash any soap on him when I gave him my tray.

I'm not talking about pity here. I'm not sure pity is appropriate for human beings to feel toward one another and I'm not sure we have the right to feel pity. Pity is more seemly when it is felt by God. But it seems to me that Adam violated a trust here. I don't think he knew it. I think he thought he was acting in the best interests of all for whom he was responsible. But I think what tripped him up was that old cultural prejudice that the drunk is always wrong. I mean, Meow Man had made a place for himself and Nacio was new. Meow Man performed efficiently in the kitchen and looked respectable when he went for a walk through the neighborhood, while Nacio was punkie and this had predisposed Adam against him, but if Nacio had stayed around a while longer, his blood sugars would have stabilized and he would have adjusted to his new circumstances. No, the bottom line is that Nacio was drunk and Meow Man wasn't. So in spite of the fact (if you will accept such an outmoded term as fact) that Meow Man was subject to dangerous manic frenzies which could be provoked by a soap bubble, Nacio, though he eluded the ice pick, was given the axe.

Surely, Nacio needed discipline. He had come to Sally's seeking that. Surely, the flying scroll cleanses the land of thieves and perjurers, but just as surely, the Mighty and Righteous One is very angry when those he appoints as shepherds add to the calamity.

This means I couldn't see what Adam had gained by sending Nacio into the wilderness except a weirdly lunar kitchen. But Adam was partly right, too. He didn't call the police. Had they come, I believe that someone besides Meow Man would have finished the dishes that night. I mean, Meow Man, like Nacio, was our problem and we are admonished to show mercy.

I think things are just a little more complicated than that. You know, hooch has drowned a lot of good men. It's treacherous stuff, a relentless master for those whom it enthralls. Among the carnival rides at Mind-benders Park, alcohol cracks the whip. Alcohol hates you. First, it makes you dirty and crazy, and then it kills you. It is an evil and feeble worm that tells lies to be swallowed and when you swallow it, it gorges on your organs, swells, and becomes a maddened dragon. It is excrement, and it transforms you into excrement. It is distilled putrescence, a mold growing amid the dying cells of your skull and while they wither, it buggers you until you caper, yelp, and sing. It is liquid folly, this mind-mold, and yet – Solomon gave himself to folly and his wisdom remained with him. Noah whose name means "comfort" cultivated a vineyard and drank himself drunk under the covenant of the rainbow. It was water, not wine, that destroyed his world; and Jesus transformed that destroying water into wine, and on that night before he died, he made alcohol a sacrament. Augustine observed that even as it was evil to make bad use of a good thing, so it was good to make good use of a bad thing. It's funny. Origen believed that in the end, Satan himself would be saved. I wonder what he read in the dregs of the goblet of history?

SOLITUDE

For my days are consumed like smoke, and my bones are burned as an hearth. My heart is smitten, and withered like grass; so that I forget to eat my bread. By reason of the voice of my groaning my bones cleave to my skin. I am like a pelican of the wilderness: I am like an owl of the desert. I watch, and am as a sparrow alone upon the housetop.

Psalm 102: 3-7

If you are a sinner, for heaven's sake have the grace to be a cynic too.

C.S. Lewis, The Pilgrim's Regress

I didn't see much of Jay following the wedding. It's an old story. The married couple enters a new circuit around a new center, among new friends. Some few are able to retain their former acquaintances, but such exceptions only prove the rule: marriage means severance and beginning. You leave and cleave. Jay and I could have been an exception, but I didn't think we would be. During the months before the ceremony, our friendship had begun to atrophy noticeably. I was surprised though at how lonely I was. I had come to depend on Jay more than I'd realized.

In early February 1980, I'd gotten a job as a janitor at K-Mart in San Patricio. It was all Pastor Gerard's doing. The manager of the store attended our church and when Pastor Gerard found out about the opening, he arranged everything, even to telling me where to go for my interview and what time to arrive. The interview lasted four-and-a-half seconds. I introduced myself and was later told to report to work at eleven-thirty the following evening. A week later, I moved out of Sally's and into a room on Central Avenue. I stayed with K-Mart for a year,

43

which was longer than I had ever stayed with anybody except the U.S. Army. The third shift gig ended in mid-March when I was transferred to first shift in the warehouse. As a direct descendant of the robin and the rooster, I was glad of the change, but there were some things about third shift, which I savored. Those, after all, are the spacey hours.

Jay's apartment was right on the way to work, so during that month-and-a-half, I'd come by at about nine-thirty P.M. Usually he'd be downstairs shooting pool, or else talking to Betty on the pay phone in the parking lot. Sometimes we'd play a game of 8-ball, but as a rule we'd just saunter upstairs, suck a doobie and talk for a while before Jay hit the sack. By ten-fifteen or ten-thirty, I'd leave and drift through the streets until I had to be at work.

Puerto Rico, at least where I lived, locked itself in at night and went to bed early. The streets were mine. I shared them only with the wind and the moon, a sly cat or two, a cruising auto, and a few stars that were able to assert their presence dimly through that halo of voltage; which in this century, had been generated above our cities and re-enforces our boast of power and atheism by shielding us from the vacuum we abhorred and populated with metaphysics. Breadfruit, mango, and palm loomed black above the flat roofs and thrust from their sable recesses, a casual spray of silvered foliage beneath this or that favored street lamp. The dusky lawns were frosted in a shimmering twilight of electricity, and the night would ripple like a drowsy cat along my sleeveless arms.

It was pleasant as well to return to my room, exhausted at eight-thirty in the morning, as the sun trod in flame against the brazen firmament. The vigor of science fails to dispel the delusion of the sun's stately progress across the royal sky. We are creatures convinced by what we see. The rational eye seduces the analytical mind and skews our systems. The confusion of truth with beauty is the error of the formalist, even as the assertion, that definition is the tautological error of the nominalist. We disguise our conceptual warps in appeals to paradox, but the fragments we scrutinize are those we create, and the whole we reassemble is a patchwork illusion of abstracted parts. We see and think sequentially, and this distracts us like a flash of blue metal on the boulevard. Sheltered from the sun, business begins. The merchant, too, is the enemy of God, numbering, valuing, while outside solar fire polishes stucco and asphalt. He is scrupulously honest, cheating no one but himself. Philosopher, artist, craftsman, janitor, each in his sackcloth of righteousness, complains to his whispering heart, "What have we to do with thee, thou watcher of men?"

Between arrival and departure, I endured the store, acres of floor-space under a canopy of salsa suspended from ceiling speakers. There were three of us who raced mutely through that semi-chaos, regenerating order from a shambles; an order, which on the morrow would be reduced again to shambles by the fervor of those crowds that surged within its walls while we were away. Each of us knew his task and had his own section of floor. We seldom saw one another and there was no need to speak. It was here, amid this perpetual reminder of the second law of thermodynamics that I first began to wonder why Adam and Eve had to eat fruit in the garden if there was no death, or how the fall had modified the carnivores, or if Eve's travail in childbirth was evidence that she had begun to stand erect,(Romans 8:22)[15]. Of one thing, I became increasingly certain: the references to agriculture (God planting and man tending a garden) focused the events in the late Neolithic. I would slowly slip away from myself as the effects of the marijuana were dissipated by the concentration of rapid labor and my meditation upon the scripture.

Brian left for California after I switched to first shift in the warehouse. Betty commanded more and more of Jay's evenings as they prepared for their peacemaking trip to the States. I had volunteered to commit my day off each week to work for a mission in Santurce, a radio-television station called WIVV, but the evenings during the week were voids in which I dangled. I would read, blow a little pot, and then prowl the <u>calles</u> during the darkling hours, until moon and lamp scorched to soot the cobwebs of my exile, and flooded my hollow dust with their cratered primeval radiance. Reverie and the rhythm of my shoes brought me into a narrow tranquility of self-absorption. I saluted the houses with my peace, but my peace returned to me.

This desert of mirrors, which I had entered, was unanticipated and I found the vista it presented in the weeks that stretched before me appalling, and in large measure inexplicable. When joining the church, I had been told that there was little of the familial concern and companionship, which one might expect from a worshipping community. A community professing itself to be called from all eternity, and for all eternity, and justly claiming an endurance record across four thousand years of history (even the Hindus couldn't claim that), four cosmological paradigms (at least in the west), and three to six covenants (depending on how you counted them). Indeed, when I left Sally's for twelve days at the end of April and the beginning of May in 1979, I tried my faltering hand with National Surfacing. After I lost the job, I confessed along and in a rented room, my love for, and sin against Jesus, and my belief in him as Lord and Savior. I had begun, during a week of seclusion, to read the New Testament and pray. I did not feel forsaken. Instead, I felt what I can only describe as a tangible presence, a presence that caused me to see my previous life in terms of forsakenness.

In the summer of 1962, my family moved from Irving, Texas, to Miami, Oklahoma. It was an easy walk to get downtown from the Terrace Apartments where we lived. It was a trip I made with increasing frequency, until we moved to Milwaukee, Wisconsin, at the end of 1964. During the summer of 1963, I became an incidental witness to the decomposition of a cat, which one night in the early part of that summer, had been struck and killed as it slipped across the road on whatever errand had prompted it to its doom. All summer long, the cat slowly dissolved into the asphalt. By the end of the summer, there was nothing to mark where the cat had died but a smear. No one who might have noticed that smear could have guessed that it had once been a living leaping cat. It looked more like a tire skid or a scuff of oil. As I passed one summer afternoon and September, peered around the edges of August, the cat-smear tripped something in my imagination and I suddenly had what I best can describe as a vision. I saw, and then became, the cat as it had crouched on the shoulder of the road and then sprinted out in front of the heedless car. The cat, bristling with its purpose, had been cancelled in an instant, and in that instant the nothingness, which had become the cat pointed at and pierced my fragile soul. This was my first existential encounter with my own finitude and it rocked me to the depth of my being. I, who had dreamed myself wealthy, awakened to find that I was wretched, pitiable, poor, blind, and naked. It was a discovery that numbed me, and one with which I discovered that I could not cope. My secular concepts were simply inadequate. The future by which I had been justified had, in that moment, been snatched away from me.

In college, I had discovered LSD. Now I don't think LSD is something that one can really like, but it is a drug, which is potentially fascinating, and I was captured by that fascination. I gave up counting, but I suspect that I have probably tripped around a hundred times. Every trip is unique, but there is a common "acidness" of perception to them all. A perception that, for me, was like this:

The world, cosmos, universe, or whatever you want to call it, seemed to me to be an organic whole of infinite and delicate complexity, a dance of light and color defying form and incorporating all conceivable harmonies into itself. But it was all ruthlessness, this dance, as hungry fire or fractured and unwondering stone. In the midst of this dance groped man-the-distorted. Man-the-distorted was man-the-thing-gatherer, man-the-thing-maker, who by his manufacturing and amassing of things, sought to assert his superiority over other men. But what was amassed was out of place, and what was made was clumsy and crooked. It was ridiculous and became very evil for men to amass and make, for what they did, was alienate themselves from one another and from the dance. Men were not intended to be generators of love of wealth. It was by men that love was to enter the world, and the failure of men to allow this love to enter, created havoc in the indifferent maelstrom of patterned power. The vortex of the maelstrom whirled away into the cat-smear that swallowed everything. This was forsakenness.

Like many children, I was fascinated by dinosaurs. When I was in the second grade in McGrath, Alaska, in 1957, my parents gave me a copy of Roy Chapman Andrews' All About Dinosaurs and a set of the prehistoric dragons. They were gray and green, cast in hard solid rubber, and the name of each was printed in tiny raised letters along its tail or, in the case of the pterodactyl, along the edge of its wing. To help the dinosaurs adjust to their new environment, the set included a thin plastic mountain painted gray, green, and brown as well as some palm trees (flowering plants not having evolved yet). The mountain cupped a blue pond fed by a blue waterfall, so the dinosaurs could have plenty to drink. Outside the powder of the deadly glaciers, spread from the pole to the Ozarks, but inside the steamy Mesozoic bred the paddlefish, and the stegosaurus, and lifted the Appalachians as high as the Rockies would become.

Between the ages of eight and ten, I read <u>All About Dinosaurs</u> many times and Roy Chapman Andrews became something of a hero for me. In my imagination, I would travel with him to rolling windswept Mongolia and together we would wrest fossilized dinosaur eggs from the gravel of the Gobi. As I began to mature, I contemplated, from the evidence left by these terrible lizards, the passage of time, and what the import was of the incontrovertible truth; that the world as I knew it, had not always been as it now was, might become very different again, and must therefore be a rather unstable place. This spoke of change on a scale whose parameters receded before my imagination, into forever. In such a universe, nothing endured and anything was possible. But the cat-smear truncated my limitless future and the LSD revealed my forsakenness.

When I sat down to read the gospels in May of 1979, what impressed me almost immediately was the ubiquity and power of Satan, and the dependence of Jesus, evidenced as he grew weary and hungry, and could not work miracles because of the lack of faith of others. Here was the primal source of love, but it seemed that power was lacking. Not that Jesus had no power. He stilled the storm, commanded evil spirits, and spoke the dead to life. He himself triumphed over death, but to do so, he had to die. I did not doubt that Jesus was the Lord of the universe, but I could not comprehend such weakness. It was Satan who I needed to defeat by the power of my love, so I set to make up for lost time and generate as much love as I possibly could, confident that this love would be reciprocated as it gladdened the hearts of men and God. I tithed, gave gifts anonymously, studied the scriptures daily with prayer (first for others, then for myself), and dedicated my one free day a week to missions. I had a prison ministry through Bob. I went to church every Sunday both morning and evening, and to mid-week prayer meetings, and I did this faithfully for seventeen months amid an increasingly mystifying solitude. In the end, I was so desperate that I quit smoking marijuana, and put the money I would have spent on that in the collection plate. But nothing helped. The tangible presence of Jesus, who was the source and spirit of love, was slowly and sorrowfully withdrawn. The rich fellowship I had expected to enjoy was stillborn, and the Christian life I had begun in the experience of a victory to be won, became a protracted struggle, which led in the end to defeat. The impulse to drink returned and became more urgent, and I began to fall before its onslaught.

Then one November evening in 1980, the scales fell from eyes. It was raining when I left K-Mart. It was not a hard rain, but it fell steadily. From the appearance of the plastered vegetation, and the swirling water that had begun to overflow the curbs, and long since washed debris from the streets, I could guess that the storm was vast and lingering. I slogged home, growing soggy under the tepid, peppering drizzle. My room was over a mile from the store, but I usually enjoyed the walk. However, having no raincoat, I soon found myself chilled by the tropical gusts. The rain, starred my glasses, blurred my vision behind a riffling lamina of shifting and running images. Cars swooshed warmly by spattering the sidewalk and leaving a wake of dank fumes. The wetter I got, the less likelihood there would be of anyone offering me a ride even if I should stick up my thumb. Somehow, the thought depressed me.

On the corner of the block where I lived, was a <u>repostaria</u> called Los Pinos Nuevos. I stopped to buy a Cubana sandwich and a bottle of Malta for supper. This was something of a splurge for me, since I was reluctant to spend any more than was absolutely necessary for my personal needs so that I would have that much more to give to the Lord's work, but the rain was so oppressive; I was tired, and my spirits flagged, so I thought a treat might be justified. Under my door, I found a letter from my mother. I changed into dry clothes and lay back in my bed, the head of which was by the window. There was no glass in the window. Instead, it was equipped with aluminum slats that could be closed or opened by turning a small handle in one corner. This was a good arrangement, since it allowed for plenty of ventilation. I rolled the slats opened slightly and felt the damp air against my cheek that was still chilly from the walk. I leaned back on the pillow, which I had propped up against the wall, opened the sandwich and the Malta, and began to read the letter. Outside, the rain chuckled and the cars on the street one floor below sloshed past. I chewed and read.

The letter was cheerful. My brother, who was living in Des Moines, was hoping to be able to go on a trip with his friend to the Andes in a few months to do some mountain climbing. My mother and father were planning to take a week's vacation over Christmas and visit Williamsburg, Virginia, and Washington D.C. Everyone was joyful and vibrant, and life during the eighth chapter of Revelation had shown a surprisingly benign face. I finished my letter and looked at my room.

The room had a single bed, a chest-of-drawers, a refrigerator, a chair, and a bed table, which was painted pink, and which I was able to fit at the foot of the bed. There was space for nothing else. I could walk in, walk out, and turn around. Six shirts, two pairs of jeans, and a pair of slacks hung from a pipe in the naked cubby-hold of a closet that gaped between the chest-of-drawers and the refrigerator. The plaster walls were painted white. In the corners, the paint had flaked away revealing an older layer of green and white. To the door, I had tacked a poster of a flying saucer descending upon a grassy, daisy-freckled hill. A boy and girl holding hands were running toward it. In the distance was the sea. I stared at the room for some time. My mind dominated by one thought: This is not the victorious life.

It did not occur to me at the time that the failure might lie with me, that the love I strove to generate, precisely because it was love I strove to generate, ceased in short order to be love's love and so ceased to be love. It did not occur to me that there were those in our community who perceived me as being arrogant and hostile. It did not occur to me, an overweening spiritual pride. Instead, I thought that the fault lay with the church, that they had not loved me enough (as if God had called his church together for the purpose of loving me). They were a clay vessel, which had failed to appreciate fully the treasure with which they had been entrusted (a treasure, which dazzled me with its promised) and so had, as I termed it, "made their deals with the world." Matthew 23[16] appeared to me in a new light. How could the people in those pews read those words and not realize that Christ was talking to them?

Yet God had not deserted me, and it was his Spirit that had wrung from me the admission that this life of generated love, which wore me out, was not the victorious life, that, indeed, the tawdry room represented a judgment upon that life and that I would perish with my money if I refused to repent. I had, as it were, given all I possessed to purchase the gift of love and that sum had been utterly scorned. But God had not scorned the one who gave it and he reached toward me, the one who had given it, with an infinite compassion, which in my umbrage and my disparagement of his people, I did not notice at the time.

Now, I don't believe that life is a test. I know that scripture uses terms like test, but I'm not sure that life per se is a test. Tests are given to determine how we have done over and against a known standard. If the test is good, one should have a pretty clear idea at the end whether one has passed or failed. If the result surprises one; it shows that the test was poorly conceived.

What strikes me about the judgment scenes in the Bible is the element of surprise. There seems to be something almost arbitrary in the division between the sheep and the goats. Now arbitrary, is a bad word, because it suggests that there is no cause or reason for the division, but there is a reason. The sheep are those who have ministered to Jesus by ministering to his brothers (defined earlier in Matt. 12:50[17] as those who do the will of the Father), and the goats are those who have failed to minister. But why the word arbitrary pops out, almost before one can think it through, is that apparently neither group is aware of when they succeeded or failed, or even if there is a comparison of accumulated successes and failures. Had the goats not even presented one of Christ's own with a cup of cold water? Esau and Jacob are worth considering here. If we may believe Jesus, Jacob is one of the elect (Matt. 8:11[18]) and if we may believe Malachi and Paul, Esau is not. Yet, Jacob cheated Esau out of his blessing, and though he got his father's blessing by deception and from his mother's, not his own, initiative, yet the birthright was considered valid even after the deception was discovered. Esau forgave Jacob that wrong and the two brothers parted reconciled, though this did Esau no eternal good and gained him nothing on earth. Surely, this baffles human concepts of justice and gives us scriptural grounds for doubting life as a test. Still, I do believe that at times in our life, God will test us despite what James 1:13[19] says. God tested Abraham and Abraham passed, and that made all the difference. Now on that November evening in that room I saw that God had judged my work by fire and that it had been consumed, but what I didn't see was that he would save me as though from fire and that he would do it with a test (Job 23:10[20]). It happened like this:

Because my brothers seemed to me to be faithless, hypocritical, and unloving and to have made their deals with the world, I, too, resolved a couple of months later to compromise, to make my own deal with the world. I decided that I would drink. I did not plan to drink as I had drunk before my conversion, but I did decide to allow myself a nip or two when the urge became too strong. However, as part of this new resolution, I decided to smoke no more pot. I would not take up both the bag and the bottle. I would leave the bag lying where I'd dropped it. However, as I began to drink, I discovered that my old patterns began to emerge. The old machinery, in spite of my resolution, was being set in motion, but now the genie in the bottle snarled more than he laughed and tormented me with a legion of fears. I discovered as well that the sobriety I had begun to consider as such a burden was precious to me, but that having counted it cheap; I could not now leave liquor alone. It was as though I wrestled with a giant who drew his strength from my resistance to him and who, every time I would cast him down, would come back stronger than before. If I drank, I grew weaker. If I resisted, he grew stronger; and God seemed deaf to my supplications.

It was during this period, still attending prayer meetings every Wednesday, on one such meeting that I found that the Wesleyan Academy in Guaynabo was looking for a janitor. I thought that perhaps a change in my circumstances would produce a change in me, that the presence of Christians around me at work would provide me with the support that I needed for reasserting some sort of control of my life. I applied for the job and, due again to the influence of Pastor Gerard, was hired. It was agreed that I should submit my two-week notice at K-Mart and continue to work for them until the period was completed. This was done, and on Monday in early February 1981, I began that four-and-a-half mile walk to Guaynabo. It was always dark when I set out.

Walking is for me, a form of meditation, so it was quite natural for me to reason with myself about the state of my faith as I tramped to work. However, in a few days, this reasoning was gradually transformed into an exhortation and the exhortation went like this:

"Look, you've tried this Christian thing and it just hasn't worked. You've been sincere. You've really given it a fair shot. No one can fault you on that score. You've tried. But there really isn't any new life here. You're just the same old you, but you've been playing by a new set of rules, that's all. Of course, there were some short-term gains as would happen with any new routine you adopted, but in the end it all collapses and you're left with you. Now you've recognized this. That's good. You've always striven to be honest with yourself. Why not admit that Jesus has failed to pull this off for you and that he's failed because he isn't really God? He just doesn't have the power. He never did. You might not want to tell the people at church that you feel this way. There's no sense upsetting them any more than you've already done, and they probably wouldn't understand anyway, so if you don't want to tell them, then don't. But at least be honest with yourself. Honesty with yourself has always been your strong suit. At least show that you've still got enough integrity to admit to yourself when you've been wrong. All you have to do is say to yourself that you no longer believe in Jesus as God. Just say it to yourself. No one else but you has to know."

This exhortation, this monologue born from a debate within myself, lasted for a couple of days. Then one dark morning, I stopped walking quite suddenly and said aloud, though softly, "But that just isn't true. I don't believe that way about Jesus at all. Okay, something is wrong. I don't know what it is, but something is wrong. But that doesn't mean I want to stop being a Christian. What has my failure got to do with the Godhead of Christ? If he's a God, he is God of whatever happens to me. I still want to be a Christian." And the monologue stopped.

And then I knew that I wasn't alone, as I had thought. There were two other people there, there always had been. One was Satan, one was the Lord Jesus Christ, and lately Satan had been doing all the talking. The Lord was just waiting to hear what I would say. And I had said it. I had confessed with my lips what was really in my heart. I said who I was and whom I wanted to be; and in the silence of Satan, the Lord had answered.
And then a slow miracle began.

EUROCLYDON

But not long after there arose against it a tempestuous wind, called Euroclydon.
Acts 27:14

And when neither sun nor starts in many days appeared, and no small tempest lay on us, all hope that we should be saved was then taken away.

Acts 27:20

What can be done with fewer assumptions is done in vain with more.

William of Ockham

The greatest miracle is that miracles do not happen.

Poincaré

The Taylor Building is part of the University of Aberdeen, Scotland, where I did my Masters of Theology. It is divided into four blocks of rooms: Blocks A through D.

Block A is over by the Student Administration Centre, while Block D ends on High Street. On the first floor of Block D are the offices of the Religious Studies Department. If you had walked into that department from High Street between 1985 and 1986, you would have seen on the wall to your left as you entered the set of doors, which separate those offices from the stairwell, a large detailed map of the state of Alaska. This map was thumb tacked to a bulletin board, which was fixed to the wall. Had you stopped and studied that map, you might have noticed south of the Yukon River another large river curving through the center of the state. This river is the Kuskokwim. Had you placed your finger at the mouth of the Kuskokwim, where it empties into Bristol Bay, and traced its course northeast through Bethel, you would have, after a few inches, reached the town of McGrath. You would notice that at McGrath, the river turns sharply east, and at Medfra, branches into three rivers: the Kuskokwim and the North and South forks of the Kuskokwim. You would have noticed also, that at McGrath, a second river, the Tokatna, flows into the Kuskokwim from the southwest, and that west of the Tokatna, there rises a range of hills called the Beaver Mountains. Of course, you might have noticed none of this. Perhaps, had the area meant nothing to you, you might have passed the map with scarcely a glance. It may have seemed to you as little more than an abstraction of a territory seldom visited by those in your part of the world. Conceivably, it might have seemed a bit incongruous. "What's a map of Alaska doing here?" But when I first saw it, I paused and I have often paused since, for the map is far more than an abstraction to me.

It reminds me of Quonset huts and diesel, of a bear cub that we chained to a doghouse in our backyard, of whistles we whittled from willow stems, of mosquitoes, and of a winter silence that settled around our squeaking boots as we walked home from school; a silence that brought the stars close. For my parents took their, two children, my brother and myself, and moved to McGrath, Alaska when I was five years old!

When I pause and contemplate that map in the corridor of the Taylor Building, those are the kind of things I remember. The map is a symbol of what is and what was.

I am a journey, not a place. My life is an animal illusion of immortality day by day. I have never dwelt long enough anywhere to notice much change. I have passed through a series of static towns. I do not forget myself; it is my friends who disappear. What Hosea said of Ephraim, he might well have said of me: gray hairs are here and there upon him, yet he knoweth not. But life, whether journey or place, is brief, and it is good to see a map of Alaska, where I spent five years of my childhood, and sometimes recall that your old friends are still alive, and that it is you they have forgotten.

The role of foreigner has made us aliens and strangers on the earth. We have become sentimental and cruel. We have become haunted, although we have not yet become empty. Perhaps, I speak only of myself. Perhaps. But let us consider the idea of haunting and see if I might be talking of you as well. Let us conceive of haunting and as a breakdown in the metaphysical order, an uncontrolled and threatening intrusion of the spiritual realm at a particular place and time. The phantom is tangible and terrible, an unwelcomed and dreaded reminder of the worm-eaten thing we will become after we have been poured back into that vastness, which was when we were not. The ghost story is the symbol that reminds us of our ultimate helplessness.

We should notice, though, that it is a symbol, which has assumed different characteristics at different times. For instance, in the gothic talks of the mid-nineteenth century, haunting usually took place in the exotic somewhere else, while in the horror literature of the late twentieth century, it usually takes place in the familiar here and now. There is, I think, an historical reason for this shift in focus. Our European parents entered the world beyond Europe as though it was a chaos. They subjugated it and shaped it into European nations using European time. But the cultural soul of Europe, so carefully nurtured by Christianity for so many generations, disintegrated in the process and left a void within her children, a void which is being filled by the "oppgz". Christ, not science, is the great bulwark against superstition; and Christ, in Europe, was the Lord of a collapsing cosmology, and was jettisoned with that cosmology. He left the house empty and swept. The memory traces of defeated gods born of fire, fear, and forest entered that empty house, and began to swell, to fill it, and to bring with them their relative from the world beyond; that world which our parents had understood as chaos. The demonic was a category all but dead in nineteenth century theology. Among twentieth century theologians, it is very much alive. We can discover its resurrection in the metamorphosis of the ghost story.

But we have not only exhumed the antique horrors, we have, in our frantic efforts to prolong our experience of life, demonized our death. Death has escaped those symbols, which two hundred years ago, invested it with meaning. Then people, when they talked of health, they talked in gastrointestinal terms. Today, when people talk of health they talk in cardiovascular terms. Then the deathbed was the site of life's great culmination, where the family gathered to hear the final words of the dying one, words that were remarked upon and remembered. Today, the lover's bed is the site of life's great culmination. The elderly are quarantined. They mumble drugged and along. Wisdom has fled, for her rebuke was scorned. Today, we live and die defiantly. We dread death as we dread the solitude and sadness that settles in the room where we wait after our uncommitted lover has gone. Life in cardio-vascular and sexual terms does not prepare us for death. Instead, it distracts us with busyness until we pass away. If we are creatures of becoming, we are not fully knowable until we cease to become, but it is precisely then that most of us are forgotten. We constantly escape from our own memory. Atheism has not freed us from the judgment. Instead, it has made that judgment merciless. This is because defiance is denial, and in all life, denying assertions fail.

So we are haunted, you and I, by the ancient deities and the enigmas of tomorrow. Iconoclasm and skepticism are floating like two eagles above the body of our culture. Truth slips through our definitions. Our symbols are like maps of places we've never been. I must create my own reality by filling those voided symbols with myself. The only authenticity is personal. But I wanted to be sure that the map I was following was leading me on the way to eternal fellowship with Jesus, and not just to some form of more authentic existence. What I wanted was Jesus Christ. I wanted assurance that the changes in my life were being effected by an external and benevolent personality. It was the Holy Spirit who was to point me toward Jesus and to lead me into all truth. But what was the Holy Spirit doing?

I suppose that at this point I should introduce the Holy Spirit. Let me begin by saying that he is the third person of the Godhead. In the western tradition, where Trinitarian discussion tends to focus more on the relational aspects (or the mutual inner-penetration) of the inner-life of the Trinity, it is affirmed that the Holy Spirit proceeds from the Father and the Son. In the eastern tradition, discussions have tended to focus more on the constitution of the Trinity, and it is affirmed only that the Holy Spirit proceeds from the Father of the Son. The origins of the difference can be traced to the beginnings of the ninth century. We might suggest, then, that the Holy Spirit proceeds from the Father of the Son, and received his form from the Father and the Son, that form being discovered in the inner-penetration of Father and Son. The function of the Holy Spirit, if I may define it very broadly, is to make the will of God manifest and to constrain us to conform to that will.

Now the Holy Spirit, so defined, is a symbol, even as the map of Alaska is a symbol. This symbol of the Holy Spirit has been constructed from analogous language. The map of Alaska has been constructed from a mass of survey data. But survey data and analogous language are not exactly the same thing. Both express relationships, but if questions arise about the accuracy of the symbol constructed from survey data, one can always reconstruct the day or resurvey the area. But no one has ever observed the inner-life of the Trinity, and scripture has little to say about the dynamics of that inner-life. What is more, analogy functions as simile and the meaning of simile, to be effective, requires ritual. There are two consequences of this requirement. First, simile can become deterministic, can limit in too great a degree the truth it seeks to illumine. Second, its ritual meaning can shift over time.

As the language of art and myth, its truth content can be relegated to the psychological realm and can be used to structure the psychological realm as though analogy could be applied as principles of natural law are applied. This reduces psychology, demonizes it, which is the great sin of Docetism. Myth point stop events which are beyond space and time, while Christian doctrine, as Peter insists (II Peter 1:16; 2:3[21]), derives from events which occurred in space and time. The incarnation assures us of flexibility. It is not the events, but their significance, which we debate. Without the events, the significance becomes only a set of rigid principles. The arguments may become simplified, but they are not thereby rendered better vehicles of truth. Events qualify the inductive argument and fulfill the words of those who speak the words of God. Miracles followed Paul from Damascus to Rome, but they did not make his life easier. For the poison not to kill him, he had to be bitten by the snake.

STRAYS

And he spake this parable unto them, saying, What man of you, having an hundred sheep, if he lose one of them, doth not leave the ninety and nine in the wilderness, and go after that which is lost, until he find it? And when he hath found it, he layeth it on his shoulders, rejoicing. And when he cometh home, he calleth together his friends and neighbours, saying unto them, Rejoice with me; for I have found my sheep which was lost. I say unto you, that likewise joy shall be in heaven over one sinner that repenteth, more than over ninety and nine just persons, which need no repentance.

Luke 15:3-7

The philosophical source from which the slavery of man derives is monism. The practical expression of monism is tyrannical. Monism is the domination of the 'common,' of the abstract universal, and the denial of personality and freedom. Personality and freedom are linked with pluralism or, more correctly, externally they take the form of pluralism, while inwardly they may signify concrete universalism. Conscience cannot have its centre in any sort of universal unity; it is not liable to alienation; it remains in the depth of personality.

Berdyaev

The Lord had spoken to me before very clearly and I had begun to believe. Because this is a narrative about guidance, I would like to pause in the midst of it to tell another story about guidance and confrontation, about the rough hands and strong shoulders that bore me on this journey of rejoicing. It happened like this:
The Libreria Betania was two blocks down and one block

over from where Sally Ann policed up the rum-rotten strays and other non compos mentis. I discovered it on Christmas Day 1978 and walked past it occasionally over the next couple of months. Positioned on the corner and covering half the block, the building had the appearance of a compound or fort. It looked completely out of place in the neighborhood and puzzled me. That it was a missionary center, and that I was on a collision course with those who labored in that shadowy vineyard, I had no inkling.

When I first arrived at Sally's in early December 1978, there were three other gringos there: Adam, who was white and had studied law, James who was black and had studied chemistry, and Vic who was black and didn't seem capable of studying anything at all. James left shortly after New Year's. He got a job working in a restaurant down in Old San Juan and went back to drinking. For a while, he would come by the store and slur his words as he told us how well he was doing. Then I didn't see him anymore. I was sorry, not because he was a lost and dying man, but because he had a passion for science fiction (a passion which I shared at the time) and it was fun to talk to him when he was sober. I would put books aside and slip them to him when he came. I doubt that he paid for them. The last batch I ended up keeping for myself.

However, if James left after the New Year, there were several other gringos who arrived. One was Tom. He was white and looked and acted younger than his forty-three years. He was from the Bronx, where he had married a Puerto Rican woman. Later, the two of them had journeyed to her sunny island to build a paradise for themselves, but Tom had a taste for "schmack" and rum and came home goofing one too many times, so his Latin lover expelled him right out of the garden. If he liked to nod, then let him dwell in the land of Nod. He drifted around in the street for a while before he drifted into Sally's.

Nathan was another American. He had spent some years in the navy but otherwise was from no place in particular. Like the Athenians, he was in every way very religious. The greatest ambition in his life was to go to India. He was taller than me (I'm six-foot-one) and kept his sandy hair in a crew cut. He was very thin and very tan, and like Tom, was in his forties.

After Nathan, Brian and Jay came, so there were seven English speakers at Sally's. I was there for fourteen months and can tell you that to have this many English speakers at one time was very unusual. Indeed, in my experience it was unique. Now, this presented Captain Victor and Estavan (who actually ran the hogar at the time) with something of a problem. They wanted to reform us but we were supposed to do more than reform (although, if the truth were known, a little reform was welcomed since the success rate was not exactly astronomical), we were supposed to confess and come to a living faith. But everything was done in Español and none of us could hablar good enough to get the gist of things like Salvador, picador and arrepentirse. So, what happened was we hung around together and talked about how much fun we had raising hell out in civilian life – all except Nathan, who was prone to wander from beer, to whores, to God, and from God to India. Apparently, the Captain, Estavan, and Bob, the missionary, had discussed this problem because one evening in late February, Bob showed up with two American kids who were willing to teach us a Bible class. They were from a missionary training center in the States and were serving a year internship at the Libreria Betania. One was a boy whose name was Stan, and another was a girl whose name was Cathy. They were very rosy, green and white. Stan, when he got a chance to talk to us, told us right away that he was not there to judge us, that he himself had smoked marijuana once. That struck me as extremely funny and I began to tease him about the stoning of Stephen. I didn't know what that was about really, it was a phrase I had picked up from something Linus had said in a Peanuts cartoon years before. Stan did not think my sense of humor was very refined, though it may have been my braying laugh that put him off. In any event, this did not augur an auspicious future. Cathy, on the other hand, augured lots better, so Tom, Brian, Jay, and I agreed to attend the class. Adam, like Jay, was already a believer, but Adam, because he was studying Spanish, wanted to sit in the Spanish service. Nathan and Vic just weren't interested, fresh flesh in the picture or not.

Stan and Cathy began that Friday by teaching us Romans. The key verse in Romans, said Stan, was, "I am not ashamed of the gospel: it is the power of God for salvation to everyone who has faith." He was using the RSV. He seemed nervous at first, and did most of the talking. Cathy didn't say much but continued to augur well. When she did speak we all watched her, but we also watched her when she didn't speak, which must have made her nervous, for after a couple of months she quit coming.

Our early discussions floundered over obscure misunderstandings. We were using several different versions of the Bible, so all the texts didn't read exactly the same. I pretended to be bothered a lot by that, and strove to twist contradictory meanings out of the variations. Stan explained patiently. Tom was upset by the phrase "to the Jew first, and also to the Gentile" (he was using a KJV). Why did the Jews come first? Did God like them better? Stan explained patiently. Brian complained that Jesus couldn't be both God's son and Dave's son at the same time. Stan explained patiently.

Stan and Cathy's visits were a pleasant break in the routine of the week and we all looked forward to Friday evening. Then one Wednesday evening in the middle of March, another American kid named Eric who had worked with Bob the missionary at the Bayamon Prison, and knew Jay from there, came by and invited us to the Libreria Betania for a prayer meeting. We had all seen the outside of the building and were curious to go. Even Nathan went, observing with equanimity as he followed us out of the rejas, "What the hell, it's something different." When we got there the room where they conducted the meeting was empty except for chairs and a standup piano. Nathan sat down at the piano and started to play. He was rusty, but obviously knew what he was about. We were amazed. After a few minutes, Nathan got up and walked over to the chairs. Shortly after that, the meeting began. Nathan left Sally's in July, Captain Victor having given him a ticket to New York. He never referred to the piano and never said anything about where or how he had learned to play. Sally's was odd like that, a dim cave filled with the gleams of what could have been or use to be. One guy named Basilio could take dictation in French. Adam, who knew French, swore up and down that it was so. Another beneficiary was an ex-boxer. Another had owned his own business in New York. Nebuchadnezzar ate grass. The grass withereth, and the flower therof falleth away.

These meetings were conducted every Wednesday and we had a standing invitation to attend. I would occasionally go, but Jay and Brian went every week. I did, however, agree to read any books the missionaries might suggest, and Bob brought me several. Most were fluff and kind of silly. I mean, you knew the world wasn't like that. It's like; maybe you shouldn't take drugs if the posters in the spirit of "Beware the Friendly Stranger" don't convince you. Instead, it's the sort of thing you pass around at parties. Lots of these books were like that kind of poster, but a couple of them really caught my attention. One was <u>Mere Christianity</u> by C.S. Lewis. The other was <u>Encounter with God</u> by Morton Kelsey. I talked with Adam about most of the books Bob passed to me, and we would laugh at some of them, but those two stayed with me. I found the Bible difficult, though, and didn't read it much at all. Things rocked along pretty quietly until well into April. Then Brian got converted.

I was a little surprised and found the whole thing kind of humorous. Brian was tough, jiving, and abrasive. He was from L.A. but had meandered to Florida where he had spent a year in prison for breaking into a store. Upon being released, he drifted back west until he reached New Orleans. There, he settled in for a bout of prolonged drinking. One day, while he was in a somewhat abstracted state of mind, he contrived to stow away on a cargo ship bound for various ports in the Caribbean. He was caught on the second day out and tossed into the brig. When the vessel reached San Juan he was put ashore. He had just enough money in his pocket for either a meal or a bottle of rum. Because he could tell that his new situation was rife with problems, which were going to require a great deal of serious thought, he bought the rum and settled down on a park bench to consider what he should do. A couple of days later, he knocked at the rejas of the <u>Hogar Esparañza.</u>

Christianity made Brian a lot easier to get along with. It "improved" him, and it started to improve him right away. For one thing, his jive began to turn into scripture. He discovered Job, and was fascinated. He began to talk to me a great deal about "good old Job." He seemed to feel that I needed very much to read this book. Once, at an evening praise session which Estavan arranged on the spur of the moment, Brian raised his hand when Estavan asked if anyone wanted to read a passage of scripture. Estavan was pleased that someone was getting into the spirit of the evening. We had already mumbled through a couple of Spanish songs accompanied by Eduardo's guitar, and it was time for the English mumblers to be edified. Estavan beamed and told Brian to read, and Brian did, wading his way through the King James Version of the hundred and nineteenth psalm.

One morning in the store I found Brian busily arranging the book section over which the Captain had given him responsibility. The Captain had put him in charge of this section for the exact reason that there wasn't much to do, for Brian took a perverse kind of pride in being lazy. Indeed, vago was one of the few Spanish words he knew. I asked Brian why he was working so hard, and he answered my question by posing another. He wanted to know if I had ever read about the sluggard in Proverbs. No, I admitted, I hadn't. "Well," Brian said, "if you had, you'd know. I don't want to be like that." And he continued to be a hard worker.

Brian began to preach sporadically. By this time, Tom had left for New Jersey, where he had family. Nathan was working with Laundries Man, and Adam was spending a lot of time in the front of the store with the Captain. Jay left right after Brian's conversion and went to work for National Surfacing. That left Vic and me. Now, Vic was not an inspiring audience. He could sit without moving for a very long time and stare at one thing. Of course, such ability would have distracted any speaker, but it was the things he said as he stared which made this peculiarity more disconcerting than it might have otherwise been. For example, on one occasion as Brian was getting into a rambling proclamation about Genesis 1:1[22], ("It says here that God created. I mean, can you imagine that? God, you know, God…created…"), Vic observed in his slow thick voice, "Some people say James Brown can sing. I don't think he can sing. The boy can dance but he can't sing." The upshot was that mostly

Brian preached to me. I took such exhortation in better or
worse humor depending on my mood.

If anyone was gospel-proof, I figured it was me. For many
years, I had been a convinced, though by no means
militant, atheist. Later, I came to believe that religious
questions were pointless, that God might or might not
exist, but if he was or if he wasn't, it was all one to me.
Lots of people thought he did exist. That was fine with
me. Lots of people admitted that they didn't know. That
was okay, too. Lots of people said he didn't. Well, as long
as they didn't act like nihilists or communists, who cared?

I was, however, impressed with the change in Brian. His
sincerity was transparent and his excitement was real. I
was also impressed by Stan. I knew he didn't like me,
that he found me repellant and irritating. Needless-to-say,
I enjoyed his discomfiture and delighted in baiting him,
but he kept coming back, kept trying to explain to me. He
was there every Friday. Now, he didn't have to put up
with it. Tom, like I said, was gone. He, Brian and Jay
could have met somewhere else or asked me not to
attend the sessions. But Stan didn't do that. He kept
talking to me, taking even my most frivolous questions
seriously. One Saturday afternoon, after I'd drunk a half
pint of Palo Viejo, I interrupted his lunch, storming into
the dining area at the Libreria Betania to badger him with
some off-the-wall query. Then, when he confessed that
he had no idea what I was raving about, I sneered at his
stupidity and, turning on my heel, stalked out proudly in
front of his peers, as though in triumph. The next Friday
Stan was there. We turned to Romans and went on with
the lessons. I could tell that what this guy had to relate to
me, he considered very important.

Now, when Jay had gone to work for National Surfacing,
he had moved into Carl's church and he continued to live
there until he got to his own place in June. At the end of
April there was an opening on the crew and Jay, with

Bob's help, contrived to get me hired. On Sunday after church, I moved out of Sally's and took a room at Los Lomas, and bought a bottle of rum for myself in order to celebrate my new freedom. The rum and I spent a very pleasant evening looking down on the people in the street. I showed up for work on Monday morning, not too much worse for wear. Now at this time in my life, I was a spaceman. I wore my hair over my shoulders, had a golden earring in my left ear, boasted a goat-tee, dark glasses, which an Army optometrist in Korea had prescribed for me when he peered into my marijuana glazed eyes, and a brightly patterned scarf, which I tied around my head. My employer believed in the entrepreneurial virtues, subscribed to the <u>National Review</u> (he went to the Wesleyan Church and would occasionally give me copies of this magazine), and was a man of many opinions. When he agreed to hire me he said, "I don't like your looks, mister, and I don't want you on my payroll, but Bob here says you're okay, so if you're not, it's Bob who looks bad."

Bob must have looked bad, because on Thursday evening, Desi (my employer's name) told me I was through. That he had never before met anyone as stupid as I was, and that he thought I was probably a liar as well as being stupid, since I had told Bob that I had a college degree. But a person as stupid as me would have had enough sense not to have purchased a degree from a diploma mill. I apologized for being stupid, explained that the work was very new for me (he interjected that work was probably a very new experience for me), and begged him to give me one more chance, that on Friday he would see a big improvement, because I was starting to get the hang of things. He agreed, reluctantly, to give me one more day. On Friday evening, he took me aside and said that he had noticed no improvement, that as near as he could tell I was as stupid as I had been on Thursday. But if I wanted to come in on Monday, he supposed I could, since he guessed that he was going to be stuck with me for a while. I thought about this all weekend. The only time he ever smiled at me was on Monday, when I came in and told him I was not going to be able to work for him anymore. He not only smiled at me, he thanked me. He even offered to drive me home. I told him I would rather walk.

Now, I had a problem. Estavan and I had started to not get along as well as I would have liked. Part of the reason was that while I was at Sally's I had started to slip out of drinks on the weekend and Estavan had caught me twice and had told me that he was going to be watching me and if he caught me again it would be evidence of my insincerity and I would be out. This was, as I have mentioned earlier, pretty standard policy. But part of the reason was more mysterious to me. It had to do with a contradiction about his childhood in which I had caught him. Twice, as we drove through San Juan, he had pointed to the house where he was born, but on each occasion, he had pointed to a different house. I asked him about that on the second occasion, and he assured me that I was mistaken, that the house he had indicated the first time was the house where he grew up, not the house where he was born. It might have been my imagination, but it seemed to me that, since that had happened he was noticeably more hostile to me. I had the distinct impression that he wanted me gone. Therefore, I was reluctant to return to the Salvation Army. On the other hand, although I had a week's wages coming from National Surfacing, I wasn't sure that the money would cover a ticket to Florida should I choose to leave the island. Besides, even if I got to the mainland, where would I go? The room I rented was paid up for two more weeks and my check from National Surfacing was due on Wednesday, so I sat, and drank, and worried for the rest of Monday and all day Tuesday. On Wednesday, after drinking a glass of rum and water for breakfast (rum and water is what the pirates called "grog"), I went back to work, said hello quickly to everyone, picked up my check, and going to the bank I discovered that, without an account, I couldn't cash it. The best thing to me seemed to be to go home and finish the rum, and see if maybe the bank's policy would have changed by Thursday. However, Thursday came and went, and I began to see that it was very unlikely that the bank policy would change anytime soon. What I needed was help. The only person I could think of who might be willing to help was Bob. Bob had always been nice to me and had seemed willing to help on other occasions. I liked him fine and thought that he probably liked me, which would excuse my bothering him with this problem, so I gave him a call and explained things to him, and he told me to meet him at the church. Los Lomas is close to Guaynabo, maybe twenty minutes if you walk. I waited for Bob under a mango tree in front of the church, and after I'd been there for maybe fifteen minutes, Bob pulled up.

Apparently, Desi had ragged Bob about my having quit, for Bob was not pleased with me. He seemed to feel that I had really made him look bad. However, he dismissed the subject in the middle of my rambling self-justification. He had come to help, he said, not to criticize. He drove me to his bank and cashed my check against his account. Before he handed me the money he made me promise not to spend it on booze, and I promised. It was a small thing to do to make him happy and I'd lied before so what did it matter? Then Bob drove me to his house and took me into a tiny study, which he had built onto the back of his garage. We sat down and he began to talk about Calvary, sin, judgment, and death. As I listened, it occurred to me that Bob was saying good-bye. This evangelical pitch defined our relationship. There could be no more. "This is your rap." I interrupted him. "This is all you've got. It's how you start and end. You're saying good-bye."

"Yes," Bob said, "I suppose that's true. If you call me again, I'll be glad to do what I can for you, but really I have nothing to offer you but the message of God's forgiveness."

Then I began to understand that what I had perceived as friendship was, for Bob, something very different. Bob acted as a friend, not to the individual, but to the man, and he did this, not for the sake of man, but for the one who had created the man. He continued to talk about the deceit of the devil but I had quit listening. The message had become impersonal, a relic passed across two thousand years of history from a hill outside Jerusalem into a garage in a hemisphere the apostles did not even know existed. It was a harsh message, flinty enough to endure: "Be sorry for what you are, spawn of hell, and accept the judgment, forgiveness, and adoption of a God in whom you can scarcely believe. Do this now or when you die, you will be confined forever in a pit of squirming horrors."

I did not doubt for an instant that Bob, although he was not saying it in quite that way, believed this. I knew also that Stan believed it, and that this belief was the source of his persistence. For these people, the message was not impersonal. It lived in the vital core of their being and made them peculiar. In most people, there is a little eye that winks at such a message and a little mouth that smiles. That eye and mouth were winking and smiling in me then. The image of a wrathful deity seemed as out of place in this world of aeons, space, time, and evolving forms as an Olmec priest in downtown Manhattan. Still, I did not laugh. Instead, I felt a deep compassion for Bob, the kind of compassion one might feel for a deluded man whose life was controlled by his delusion, but who was able to maintain some level of normalcy in spite of his confusion. I could have no more laughed at Bob than I could have laughed at the village idiot who was trying to tell me how concerned he was that I should be slain by a dragon if I went into the forest. So I asked him what I should do. Again, I wanted to put his mind at ease. Bob told me that I should confess before him in that little room that I believed that Jesus was the Son of God, that he had come to die for my sins, and that I wanted to accept his forgiveness. So, I cooperated with Bob. I repeated the words to make Bob happy. "Sure, Bob, I won't spend this money on liquor." "Sure, Bob, I believe in Jesus and his offer of salvation and I accept it as an offer he makes to me." It was a social lie, intended to make life a little easier. And Bob said, "Hallelujah, brother, you're saved." But he sounded tired when he said it, as if he didn't really believe it. As I left with my money and a craving for the rum it would buy, I knew that I couldn't blame him because I didn't believe it either. My confession was a form as empty as Bob's message. I might as well have kissed the Bible and asked God to take away a wart.

THE VOICE

Oh that I might know where I might find him! That I might come even to his seat! I would order my cause before him, and fill my mouth with arguments. I would know the words which he would answer me, and understand what he would say unto me...Then the Lord answered Job out of the whirlwind, and said, Who is this that darkeneth counsel by words without knowledge?

Job: 23:3-5; 38:1-3-7

If, for example, feeling is the essential organ of religion, the nature of God is nothing else than an expression of the nature of feeling...feeling is absolute, divine in its nature..."God is love"...only expresses the certainty which human feeling had of itself, as the alone essential, i.e., absolute divine power, the certainty that the inmost wishes of the heart have objective validity and reality, that there are no limits, no positive obstacles to human feeling, that the whole world, with all its pomp and glory, is nothing weighted against human feeling...God is the nature of human feeling, unlimited, pure feeling, made objective...The fundamental dogmas of Christianity are realized wishes of the heart; the essence of Christianity is the essence of human feeling...Emotion is the Paraclete of Christians.

Feuerback, The Essence of Christianity
The truth is a very difficult thing to tell. People who think it's easy to tell the truth have never tried. They may have told some small truth, as if it was they who chopped down the cherry tree, but they have never tried to tell their personal truth. This is the truth that is hard to tell.

Part of the problem is that we don't notice everything that's happening even when it's happening around us, and we forget more and more of what we noticed as the event becomes distant. The mind creates a continuous fabric from a series of instantaneous impressions and recalls, not the impressions, but the created fabric. The very conviction of the eyewitness makes him unreliable. Our life is made up of such half-remembered, partially perceived events and, of course, we cannot be objective and we cannot play events over again or conduct experiments with alternative scenarios. What happens is, and is snatched away forever. We live as incidental beings on the periphery of a continuum of objective events and we live at the centers of our own imaginary universes. It is as peripheral beings that we amass the data, which brings texture to our imaginary worlds, but it is as beings that have a central role in imaginary universes that we abstract conclusions and invest those conclusions with significance. We perceive as worms; we remember as gods. Why some events should seem more significant than others remains, as often as not, inexplicable and behind our ascriptions of significance and within our desires looms the subconscious. Freedom and objectivity are ideal states. Human truth is something else again.

I say this by way of caution for the next few pages, like this entire frog-stimulated story, is the account of a subjective revolution, which I can recall only in part, and which I distort in my attempt after so many years to record objectively. Psychological processes, like living organs, are not intended to be abstracted from those dark environments where they work. Only when they are dead can they be dissected and such dissection always makes them appear grotesque. However, there is much to be learned by observing the organ when it is pickled, prodded, and sliced, so, although I cannot tell the truth, I propose to tell as much of a truth as I can encompass in these few pages.

Now, I was still kind of drunk when I walked away from Bob's house and I was also kind of sad. This was, I thought, the watershed of our relationship. Never again would I look on Bob as a friend upon whom I could call if I needed help. How selfish we are. It was Bob's altruism that put me off. A deed in the name of friendship was gratefully received, but I could not accept the same deed in the name of charity. What divided us was a question of faith. It was this faith that made our friendship impossible for Bob, and yet, required him to respond charitably toward me. As this reality began to emerge from the misty feelings I was sorting through, it sparked in me a sense of hostility, and realizing this hostility, clarified for me an aspect of my feelings toward Christianity. It occurred to me that I was not a little hostile toward the Christian message, and this hostility, as it registered with me, puzzled me. I could not figure out why I was so antagonistic to believing that Jesus was who Bob said he was. In the first place, I had no proof one way or the other about Jesus. My assertion that Jesus was not God was as much a faith-statement as Bob's assertion that he was God; and faith-statements were beyond proof, so my hostility could not be a consequence of some fear I might have of being wrong and so appearing foolish. In the second place, these people had never done me any harm. They seemed mildly eccentric, but they were likable. Indeed, I actually enjoyed their company. They wanted me, so I reasoned, to join a fan club—a fan club of which they were enthusiastic members: the Jesus Christ fan club. Yet, I was antagonistic to this fan club, and my antagonism bothered me. My pride was stung. I had always boasted that I was open to new experiences, that I was not prejudiced, and that if the opportunity presented itself, I would try almost anything once. Or even more than once. If these people had wanted me to join the Batman fan club, I would have probably done so for a lark. I would have read the comic books and sported the paraphernalia of Batman, if only for a while. Why then was I not willing to join the Jesus Christ fan club for a few weeks and see what happened? Something C.S. Lewis had written began to niggle at my mind. Try it for just six weeks, he had said, if there's nothing to it, you'll know. Suddenly, as I was walking along, I was tempted—strongly tempted—to try this thing. I could be as sincere as I knew how to be. I could ask Jesus to come into my life, and if he came; okay, I would have to deal with that. If he didn't; okay, I would have to deal with that too, but either way, I would know. In my knowledge, these people would be revealed to me. I would know what they were and such knowledge would be god-like. If nothing happened, it wouldn't do for these people to tell me that I hadn't been sincere – I would know I had, and I would know without a doubt as I looked into their serious intent faces and listened to their pious words, that they were real, or (as I suspected) that they were not. The veil was waiting to be ripped back and I would know. I would know. In my heart I would know. It was a temptation I could not resist. To be able to see that little eye that winked in them and that little mouth that grinned, even as it winked and grinned in me. While outside our big placid faces stared at each other and we droned on and on, planets of empty words orbiting two grinning winking suns, why it would be like an LSD trip every time I entered church. So, I went for it; I went for it big. But it all hinged on my own sincerity. For if I was not sincere, there would be no perception. But I knew that at that moment, I was perfectly willing to be sincere. So, I stopped and looked up at the blue sky, that same blue sky that had swallowed Sartre's god, and I said, "Okay Jesus, if you're real, I'll give you six weeks to prove it. I'll try, just as seriously as I can, to believe in you, but if at the end of six weeks there's nothing there, then I don't want to hear any more." When I did this, I was quite pleased with myself, with my sterling character, with my willingness to be opened to another experience, with my having given Jesus such a fair chance. Six weeks! Will you plead for Baal? Will ye save him? If he be a god, let him please for himself. The sky, of course, said nothing.

When I got to my room I felt hungry, so I went to a pizzeria and purchased a small pizza and a six-pack of Corona. I thought, considering my new status, that I ought to do something religious, so while I ate, I read the gospel of Mark because it was the shortest and would give me some idea of what the gospels were all about. It was such a sterile experience that in the next few weeks, I forgot that I had read Mark on that day, and began to believe that my Bible reading began on Sunday. But the truth was that I read Mark that Friday as I licked up bits of greasy cheese and swallowed slugs of sour and warming beer, and Mark said nothing to me at all. He remained impassive as the sky.

When I awoke on Saturday, I was very anxious, not about God or anything spiritual but about what I was going to do in the immediate future. I had over a hundred dollars. I didn't know whether I could get a ticket to Miami with that but I figured I ought to find out where I stood, because if I couldn't afford a ticket, then in large measure, my problem would be reduced to one choice: I would have to brave Estavan and ask if I could go back to Sally's. It was early and I had all day, so I decided to walk to the airport and see about prices. To walk there and back would take the better part of my day, so I had a few swigs of rum from a bottle that I had on my dresser (sobriety had nothing to do with sincerity, the two categories were, for me, quite distinct) and left. The day was sultry, dank, hot and cloudy. I stopped and bought a bottle of Lancer's to help me on my way.

As I was walking along, sipping the wine, I met one of the American missionary kids from the Libreria Betania. His name was Larry and he was going into the hardware store. We waved at each other and he smiled, though he must have seen the red pottery bottle, for I made no effort to conceal it. I continued on, thinking about Larry not at all. Now, this next part is foggy to me. After all, I'd had no breakfast, except some rum and this bottle of wine. But as I came to the bottom of the wine, I discovered that I had become very tired. I supposed that it was because of the oppressiveness of the day, and maybe because of the alcohol. In any event, my steps grew shorter and slower and the road to the airport seemed to stretch into the far distance. I decided that I wasn't going to be able to make it, that it would be better to try in the morning, after I'd had a better breakfast. However, as I returned to Los Lomas, my energy levels rose and my stride grew quicker and stronger. I walked for some time. The street was busy. I have no idea how I noticed Larry when he drove past. But notice him I did, and suddenly, without thinking about it at all, I raised my arms and started waving at him. He saw me and pulled over to the curb. I climbed into the front seat and, reaching into my pocket, shoved all my money at him. He took it in amazement. I burst into tears and started to babble. I told him that I was sick of the life I was living, that I didn't want the money because I would just spend it on liquor, that I would do anything he told me to do, even cut my hair if it would help me sober up. Then I stuck my head out of the car window and vomited down the side of his car. He took me to the Libreria Betania and, with Stan and Eric who appeared together from somewhere, led me into a backroom and prayed with me, gave me a Bible to read, and left me. I don't remember if I rinsed my mouth out or cleaned up at all. I do know that I stayed in the room for quite a while. They told me a long time later that they had looked in on me occasionally and had seen me reading and praying, but I remember nothing of that. I do remember pacing back and forth in the room and lying on the cool tiles because I felt like I was roasting. Occasionally, I thought about the money I had given Larry and this worried me, but later I decided, "Forget it, he'll probably give it back and even if he doesn't, so what? I've been broke before, and anyway I can always go to Sally's." Coherency slowly returned and with it embarrassment. I had totally blown my cool.

Of course, they had not locked me in, so after I had pulled myself together sufficiently, I left the room, accosted one of the missionaries, and told him that I was sorry for the disturbance I had caused and that I was leaving. He told me to wait for a moment and disappeared into the store, returning quickly with Larry, Eric, Stan, Cathy, and several other American kids, all as wholesome as Wonder bread and as white as the snows of Minnesota. I felt like a dirty rag among clean linen napkins. Larry returned my money (which didn't surprise me) and they all expressed concern and kept asking me how I felt, if I was all right and that sort of thing. I made noises like "Sure, sure I'm okay" and "You guys are really terrific" and using this as a smokescreen, was able to escape.

Now, what had happened was not a major disaster for me. Doper behavior can be extreme, it comes with the territory. I mean, where is it written that drug abuse makes you nice? I've never stripped myself naked in public or stood in the middle of the street and tried to direct traffic, but I know people who have. I can tell you that waking up in a room with a Bible and going out of an unlocked door to confront missionaries is not nearly as bad as waking up in a jail cell and having to kick on the bars and shout until some cop comes to tell you why you're there. So, I was not overly concerned about this incident. It was an embarrassment but one I could get over fairly quickly.

When I reached my room, I was no longer particularly hungry, but I did finish the rum on the dresser and threw the bottle away on my way out for a walk to enjoy the evening. The shadows were cool and pleasant. Larry had returned my money. I couldn't see that I was any worse off than I had been in the morning. As the traffic thinned in the streets, I returned home and went to bed filled with a sense of relief.

I awoke before dawn, feeling as though something huge was crawling around in me and trying to burst out of my skin. The peace I had known had been oxidized by my liver. It occurred to me that my liver was becoming an expensive problem. It seemed bound and determined to rid my system of every joyous chemical I injected. Like an irritable child, my body grumbled against this quisling in its midst.

I left for church and arrived far too early, but the door was unlocked so I went inside. There was no one in the sanctuary, so I went downstairs and saw Pastor Gerard coming out of the men's room. When he saw me he looked surprised, then smiled a pastoral smile. "Good morning," he said.

I was nauseated and my brain felt numb. Normally, I would have growled, "What's good about it?" Instead I found myself growling, "What's heaven like?"
"I don't know," he responded. He was all sincerity. "But I'm sure God has something wonderful planned for us."

How could one argue with an answer like this? Besides he obviously needed to prepare for the service. Schedules left us no time to explore the metaphysical implications of a life spent to acquire a berth in the hopefully wonderful hereafter. So, I grunted blearily and blinked my strawberries at him and he left, though it seemed to me that his smile had become a little fixed.

The morning fluttered past in a disconnected series of shattered images. I could not concentrate on anything. I was consumed by thirst but drank no water for fear of vomiting. I was sickeningly hungry. I slipped into the men's room a couple of times to wash my face. The day was overcast, which was a blessing, for the clouds blunted the terrible spears of light. After the last hymn, I slunk from the church. A couple of drivers saw me on the road and asked me if I wanted a ride, but I declined. I was starting to feel a little better. The walk to Los Lomas seemed to be clearing my head, but there was still a lot of smoggy turmoil between my ears. I could not decide whether I should ask Estavan if he would allow me to return to the Salvation Army, or whether I should fly to Florida. I went up to my room and began to change into the jeans and shirt I wore yesterday. The conundrum struck me as absurd. I had been over this ground again and again and still couldn't decide what to do. What was the use of God if he couldn't give me some guidance in such a simple decision? The obviousness of the thought was almost startling. Had I even asked God? As I put on my shirt I said, "Look, God, I need to know what I should do. Do you want me to go to the Salvation Army or do you want me to fly to Florida? I don't have a whole lot of time. I don't have a whole lot of money and I'm out of work. The longer I wait, the less money I have. That's how things work down here. I need to know quickly what I should do. Should I stay or fly?" And I continued to button my shirt. That was when God spoke to me.

I say God spoke to me. I mean that I understood the voice to be divine. I say "the voice," but I do not mean that my ears registered any sensation. It was more like mind was speaking directly to mind. The words conveyed an imperative. I stood completely still with my hands on my buttons and a stupid grin on my face. The voice said, "Wait a minute. You don't turn your life over to me and then set up a dichotomy and tell me to choose. I don't want you to go to the Salvation Army and I don't want you to go to the airport. You've got a room here for another week and enough money so that you won't starve. I want you to lie down on your bed, take your Bible out, and start reading it. I want you to get to know me."

In my church it was quite common for people to say that God had spoken to them about this or that. I had always thought that this was just a way of talking about intuition or something similar, but after the voice had finished I thought, "So, that's what everyone has been referring to." The Bible was lying on the bedside table where I'd left it after reading Mark on Friday evening. I stepped over to the bed, picked it up, and lay down. I then turned to Matthew and began to read. The gospel leaped to life. This was the most gripping story I had ever read, and I never doubted for a moment that the events described were actual events, even though what Jesus said and did was not what I would have expected God to have said and done. And Satan! Why the power of Satan was awesome. It seemed to me as if the entire world was in the grip of a horrible creature. I was stunned, then dismayed. I had never believed that Satan existed, but when I pictured him, I thought of him either as a romantic rebel (an image I had picked up from Milton's "Paradise Lost" when I was in college) or else as a Hamilton Burger to Christ's Perry Mason, with me as the defendant and god as the judge. I suppose had I carried the analogy further, I would have assumed that Burger and Mason (or Satan and Christ) would sit down after the case, have a cup of coffee and talk about whatever it was that cosmic beings talked about. But how different Satan appeared to me now. He seemed far more like that seedy stranger who invites a child into his car, gives the child a stick of candy, takes the child for a nice ride and later another little body is discovered raped and butchered in a field somewhere. This was no romantic rebel or judicial adversary. This was evil and hatred and pathology in personal form, and I had danced quite cheerfully to his tune for his fay music was everywhere. It was in the winking eye and the smiling mouth. It was in the righteousness of the Pharisee and the sinfulness of the publican. It was in the criminal, the patriot, the lawyer, the traitor, the farmer, the craftsman, the king, the servant, the judge, the parent, and the child. Every foot responded to this merry and terrible voice that called the numbers in a diabolical cotillion where the dead changed partners with the dead. That the world could be this way made the most perfect sense to me, and that I had never seen it before was ghastly. I had never before understood things in such stark terms, even when I saw men twisted before my eyes through the lenses of LSD. It was in seeing that everything was shot through with this terrific evil that I understood why the gospel was called good news. It was good news only because things were so bad. Before the world had been peopled with good guys, bad guys, and in-between guys. Now, it was filled only with the lost and found; and in each of the lost, a little eye winked and a little mouth smiled, and by winking and smiling, encouraged the conceit that each one of them, no matter how depraved they behaved, was really a being who was just and good and noble. Each one cherished the illusion that if he or she were understood, then he or she would be appreciated and loved. It never occurred to anyone that if he or she were understood, the understanding might evoke disgust, loathing, revulsion, and hatred; that understanding might be the precursor to condemnation. It never occurred to anyone that he or she was truly hideous and that love for a person so repellent might be an act of divine graciousness, or that he or she was so evil that tremendous provision would have to be made to correct that evil. Yet, this was very much the perspective that sprang to life for me as I first read the gospels in that second week of May 1979. I still believe today that this perspective was substantially correct.

I remained in the room for a week and read the entire New Testament. The presence of another being in that room was often palpable. It never occurred to me to doubt that the being in the room was Jesus. Objections that I raised at certain junctures were dismissed by that presence as irrelevant for the moment, and I was instructed to continue to read. For example, the reference Jesus made to Noah recalled all my objections to the idea of a worldwide flood. How, I asked, could I believe in Jesus if I could not believe in Noah? If I couldn't accept a universal flood, that was okay for the moment, the presence said. I was to continue reading. I was a Christian, not a Floodist, and I guess that's what I've always remained: a dry land Christian.

On Tuesday morning, when I woke up, I felt constrained to write my family and some of my friends and tell them that I had become a Christian, but I didn't want to do it. Why not? The presence queried. I didn't want to answer, but finally confessed that I was ashamed of what I had done, that I was afraid that the little eyes in them would wink and the little mouths in them would smile, and they wouldn't understand what I had done. Why, I hardly understood it myself, and I had done it. "Ashamed!" Jesus said. "Then I'm ashamed of you." So, I wrote the letters.

By Thursday, I was on the phone to Bob demanding to be baptized. Jay, Brian, and I were baptized together by Bob at his home on a Sunday afternoon toward the end of May. We were immersed in water, contained in a metal coffin, which was painted white. A woman visiting from Minnesota and who had been a confessing Christians for years asked at the last minute to be baptized with us. Bob, Pastor Carl, and several others who had come from the two churches to witness our public confession, laid hands on us and prayed before we stepped into the coffin. Pastor Carl prayed in tongues. I don't recall, however, if hands were laid on the woman or if prayers were said over her, for I believe she asked to be baptized after this part of the ceremony had taken place. Pastor Gerard was away at the time and had wanted to perform the ceremony himself at the church, but because I was so insistent, so Bob agreed to do it in his home. When we changed back into dry clothes we were served cake and a glass of Coke. Bob called this communion. As we ate, we talked to one another.

During the evenings of that first week, I would go to the Libreria Betania and talk. They were excited by my conversion, and from then on, I began to attend their worship sessions regularly. We would meet on Wednesday evenings and sing choruses, and would be exhorted by one of the interns, that is, by one of the American missionary kids, or else, by one of the staff. Nothing in these meetings was changed, but now everything was different. When I closed my eyes and began to sing softly with the others, I would feel a deep sense of communion with that vast host who had sung to my Lord over the centuries in cloister, home, or catacomb. There was a sense of eternity in those songs, for one knew that the praise of God had been sung and would be sung forever.

Towards the end of the first week, I went to the Salvation Army to see about returning. When I got to the Hogar Esperañza, I discovered that two major events had transpired in my absence. First, Basilio, the beneficiary who could take shorthand in French, had died. Second, Estavan had been arrested. It turned out that Estavan's real name was Leon and that he was a wanted man. As he had been married by the Captain only a few days before, this arrest created all manner of difficulties about the status of his wife (he had been married under a false name and false pretexts). The Captain asked Adam to take over the Hogar, and Adam welcomed me back like a

long lost brother. Two weeks to the day after we had
unloaded my stuff from the Chevy Van, we were loading
it back in for the return trip to the Hogar. I remained there
with the Salvation Army until the early part of February
1980.

CLAY SUPPER

And in that day did the Lord God of hosts call to the weeping, and to mourning, and to baldness, and to girding with sackcloth: and behold joy and gladness, slaying oxen, and killing sheep, eating flesh, and drinking wine: let us eat and drink; for tomorrow we shall die.

Isaiah: 22:12-13

Suffering is not increased by numbers: one body can contain all the suffering the world can feel.

Graham Greene, *"The Quiet American"*

So, I had heard the voice. The Lord had called me to repentance, but had I truly repented? Had I tasted of Christ and, if I had tasted, had I affirmed him good? Had the manna of heaven been sufficient or did I long for the flesh pots of Egypt? It seemed to me that I had fairly exhausted my bricks before the tower I'd hoped to build was barely begun. The enemy against whom I'd marched so boldly had scattered my forces. I wondered if this was not because sin, rather than my Savior, remained my Lord and happiness.

The behavior of the convert oscillates between timidity and presumption. On the one hand, the convert is vulnerable. Having, on conversion, as much as confessed that the assumption around which he has structured his entire life have been false, he enters a period, however briefly, when he is as open as he has been since childhood. During this interim, he begins to adopt a different set of assumptions in an attempt to give what he has become a coherent identity. Most converts do not evaluate a body of doctrine before embracing it.

Instead, they reject what they were, embrace the community, which convinced them of their guilt, and then seek their identity within that forgiving community. This experience of guilt and forgiveness invests the doctrine of the community with authenticity. Christians have, for over two thousand years, sought to articulate their faith in a wide variety of ways, which means that the convert may easily mistake something very new for something very old. Because he lacks, at least initially, historical perspective, he may believe that the tradition in which he finds himself (finds himself in both senses of the term) is normative and that other traditions are less-than-adequate variations of this norm. Hence, a tradition may come to embody salvation and usurp the place of Christ as the vehicle of salvation. This peculiarity of the psychology of conversion exacerbates a tendency in the convert to adopt an almost prophetic stance, to make pronouncements so absolute that they might as well be prefaced "thus sayeth the Lord." Such a stance is encouraged in traditions which stress the immediate guidance of the Holy Spirit in all aspects of life, and which encourage (if only by example) their members to use expressions like "The Lord spoke to me" or "I was moved by the Spirit to act as I did." The church through which I had become converted was such a "Spirit-filled" body. I quickly adapted to the situation, swallowing many a doctrinal camel in the name of apostolic purity, and coughed up a few camels of my own for popular consumption. I was not so crass as to assert that I knew the truth as certainly as God knew it. But I had been converted to the truth as much as to Jesus (were not the two one?). And Jesus, who revealed himself to me, would surely continue to reveal his truth to me if I asked in prayer and read my Bible in faith. I was naïve enough to believe that the kind of wisdom and understanding I sought would come while I was on my knees, instead of when I was in the library. Such humility is the wellspring of arrogance. However, in time, my confidence was shaken.

Without my being fully aware of it, my concerns were philosophical. Such issues revolved around the problem of order, the problem of the one and the many, the problem of the particular and the universal. Those who, like me, address this problem with reference to divinity begin to do theology. Because there is no ultimate solution to the problem of order, theology, like philosophy, remains fluid. The tension which drives us to reflection is the tension of life itself. We seek to symbolize this tension by formulating abstractions about it. Conversion, by confronting me in a new way with this problem of order, had made my life far more interesting and complex than it had been before, when I had, in spite of my supposed non-conformity, donned the uniform of a subculture that remained primarily reactive. The radicalism of the "hippies" began to appear to me as a vague and seedy romanticism, and a very poor affair. Christianity demanded something of me that went far beyond good vibes and flower power. At first, I had been dismayed by my conversion, for it seemed to me that if all I did had ultimate significance, the fun of life was spoiled. Under the influence of my "Spirit-filled" community, I strove to overcome this dismay by employing my Christian belief as though it opened to me a system of ready-made solutions to this problem of constant crisis. Of course, the Bible was the source of this system, but as I attempted to structure its verses syllogistically, it produced more dilemmas than it solved. Its statements often seemed ambiguous if not contradictory. "Blessed are the peace-makers," said our Lord, (Matt. 5:9)[23], but of himself he said, "I have not come to bring peace but a sword." (Matt. 10:34)[24]. As a source of strength my church, too, had its limitations, for its members remained, in spite of their professions of saintliness, all too concerned with their middle class respectability. I sought the Lord in prayer, but the voice I had heard remained silent and prayer began to seem like a monologue in an empty room. In this way, my anxiety was transformed into suffering, and this suffering stripped me of my new pretensions and spurred me on toward Jesus. My doubts were expressions of my belief and the Holy Spirit used them, laboring, convicting me, admonishing me through my disquieted heart, pruning, and refining me. My struggle was toward mystery. It was a mystery I sought to symbolize.

I found the missionaries most unhelpful when it came to clarifying my dilemmas. Those who tried to give answers were often the ones with the worst answers to give. One man, comparing the church to marriage, went on to assert that in the world to come, there would be no church, even as there would be no marriage. "Marriage and the church are institutions," he said, "and institutions are made for this world. There won't be any communion, or baptism, or anything like that. We have them in this world, not in the next, not in the restored world. But here you should be baptized, take communion, and belong to the church, and you should be married, too, you know."

Now, this was a pretty standard rap for our church. Singleness was not considered to be wrong, but it was not deemed as God's best. Men and were made to cleave. It was part of God's plan. Children were an extra blessing to be given in God's time, but the central focus was cleaving. Two could chase more than one; two was stronger than one. That was the way God had made it. Still, it seemed to me that if the church was comparable to marriage, then the church might act as one's spouse, picking up one who stumbled, or providing strength to the weak; and I said as much.

"But they don't," the man replied. He went on, and as he talked, his voice began to grow harsh, almost strident. "And you know they don't. Evangelicals shoot their wounded. Even the Lord needed help to carry his cross.

If the church had been called over, instead of Simon of Cyrene, I imagine the procession would have stopped. The crowds, the soldiers, everyone would have gathered around to hear the sermon. The church would have stood there looking down at Jesus and would have said, "Come on now, Jesus, where is your faith? All things are possible for him who believes. Pray to God and he'll send you strength to carry that beam. Come on! Up! Up! You can do it!" The man was jerking his hands in the parody of a sermon. "That's what the church would do. The church would let you lie there. And where was Jesus going? He was going to die. The church is supposed to help you on, help you to die. But they don't. They aren't willing to get down there and pick up that beam. That's what a wife is for. You need a wife to do that. Husbands and wives help each other. They help each other on to Golgotha. They help each other to die. Your flesh is your enemy. It's your flesh you've got to overcome. But Eve was made from the rib of Adam, not from his flesh but his bone. It's the bone that supports the flesh, gives it strength, helps it to overcome itself. You need a bone."

What a harangue! I'd never thought of marriage in quite that way, and indeed, it sounded contradictory to Proverbs 31:31[25]. Still, that was Old Testament, after all, and who was King Lemuel anyway? Certainly, no Jew. Besides, his mother told him all that. I mean, what else could a mother say? Of course she'd say, "Marry a good cook." She'd never say, "Marry someone who'll help you die." But his criticism of the church, how spiritual that sounded, resembled my own, after the insight I'd had in my room.

On another occasion, I asked one of the teachers at the academy why, if the Bible was infallible, did we read in II Kings 24:8[26] that Jehoiachin was eighteen years old when he began to reign, and that he reigned in Jerusalem for three months. While in II Chronicles 36:9[27]

it says that Jehoiachin was eight years old when he began to reign, and that he reigned in Jerusalem for three months and ten days? Was he eight or eighteen? And where did those ten days come from? She told me they were two different kings. "No," I said, "their names are spelled the same."
"Well," she replied, "they are two different kings whose names are spelled the same."

"But they are one and the same king," I insisted. "II Chronicles is telling the same story II Kings is telling."
She shook her head and, smiling, excused herself, saying she was late to class. When I related the incident to Pastor Gerard, he laughed and dismissed the whole thing by saying that some people were less flexible than others were. But that answer left me more baffled than before. What did flexibility have to do with infallibility?

On yet another occasion, one of our Sunday school teachers made a distinction between repentance and contrition. "The difference, he said, was that the man who repented abjured forever the sin for which he repented, while the man who had only acted contritely was apt to commit the sin again when given the chance. "God," the Sunday school teach went on, "does not forgive contrition, only repentance."

As I was beginning to resume my old drinking patterns, (this happened right before Jay's wedding), I was deeply shaken and asked Pastor Gerard if this was true. He beamed and nodded. "Yes, that was a very good way to look at it." I think he was reacting against the assertion that had begun to raise its head in the church, that one could be a good Christian and still keep right on sinning; a camel, which I'd not coughed up, but which I was eager enough to swallow. This assertion was understood by both its defenders and its detractors to represent the sum of Calvinism. It devolved to the argument that either God was the author of sin, or else I earned my salvation. I think that Pastor Gerard saw latent in me such a Calvinist. However, that was not what I was asking about at all. I was trying to figure out, whether or not, I'd ever been saved. Was I slipping up because I only knew contrition? I pondered that question all the way home from church and deep into the hot afternoon. I thought that I'd repented, that I was done with the booze. Indeed, at the time, I had been hardily sick of it. But perhaps, I'd only been hung-over; perhaps it was just a carnal thing after all. Finally, in despair, I purchased a quart of rum and, settled back on my bed with a copy of "Moby Dick", which I was reading for the second time. I got good and drunk. There would be no church for me that evening. Such is the effect of life-giving words.

As I worked around school during the next few days, I tried to convince myself that I wanted an objective truth to be there, for I was having a problem, which I couldn't control and I wanted it solved. I was afraid of alcohol, really afraid of it. However, I could not convince myself that I was prey to desires not my own, that I was the hapless play thing of demons. My problem was a moral problem, and a moral problem was not introduced by outside agents. What was being revealed to me was the corruption of my own heart.

Addiction, I thought, is when your wants become needs. I can understand how it happens. I can understand how someone might become curious about drugs, and if the opportunity presented itself, how he might decide to give it a try. I can understand how he might enjoy or become fascinated by the effect they produce, and decide to use them for recreational or other purposes. I can understand how this might begin to define his lifestyle. I can understand how this might become a problem, and he might deny that he has a problem at all. I can understand how, at some point, he might begin to admit that he has a problem and to seek help for it. I can understand how he might be cured. All of this makes good sense to me. What I cannot understand is why, after all that has happened, after his curiosity has been satisfied, after he has discovered that the enjoyment provided by drugs was, in the end, only a type of enjoyment in a world rich with good things. How it can be very dangerous and quite short-lived, after he has suffered through the craving and the cure, and has set out in a new direction, that things take a tyrn. What I cannot understand, and yet, what I know by hard experience to be true, is why drugs could still exercise that fatal fascination that they exercise for dopers. Cure, like prison, becomes another interlude in the lifestyle of the addict. The dog returns to its vomit. It is in this return that we see a witness to Original Sin. It is here, where the desires run deepest that the struggle is joined.

I was not seeking an excuse to sin. I recognize that Pastor Gerard was right when he preached that sin was not the problem. But I didn't need an excuse to sin. I was not in sufficient control of my desires to require an excuse. My craving was its own justification. What I was looking for was a way not to sin, a way to strengthen my own feeble will. My problem was that I could not help myself.

Now, all this happened several years ago. My life is, again, under control. I have married. I have returned to school earning a M.A. in Theological Studies from Brad Graham Center, Wheaton College, Illinois and eventually my Ph.D. in Christianity in the non-western world from the University of Aberdeen, Scotland, UK. Along this way I found some answers to the questions which I asked. More importantly, I have acquired a level of perspective, which in an odd way, is often better than a straight answer. The road back to sobriety was much harder the second time, but I have gotten a complete victory over it. I have learned to treasure the beautiful gift of a clear mind that Jesus has given me. What I want to try to do in these last couple of pages is express, as clearly and briefly as I can, something of what I have learned. It is this:

There is a two-part movement that lies at the very core of Christianity. It is salvation and worship. The Christian is saved by the power of another, and in response, he worships that other, but there is more to it than that. The Christian is saved by the power of the one who suffers. In this suffering lies the real mystery of the gospel. The Christ, the man of sorrows, the suffering servant, was the incarnation of God. Jesus comes to us in our sorrow and our suffering and we worship. We know who we are when God reveals himself to us, and like Job, we quit blaming God and worship. God was not looking for Job's righteousness. God was seeking a broken and contrite heart, and when God appeared, that was what Job offered spontaneously. Good old Job. That was what Brian meant.

Jesus never tells us to love ourselves, he merely observes that we do. We love ourselves as Job loved himself. We strive to be righteous. We strive to love; and that is why we fail. Jesus does not tell us to be kind and considerate, to be nice, to be gentlemen. Instead, he tells us to love our neighbors as we love ourselves. In saying this, he points to the problem and to the impossibility of our being able to solve it. It is our love of self, which has separated us from our neighbors and from God. This inverted and trivialized love is not genuine love at all. To be genuine, love must become and remain transcendent. Empathy is the vehicle for that. In the incarnation, God has empathized with man. In Jesus we see the fullness of that empathy revealed. Through the gift of the Spirit we, too, begin to empathize. We express this empathy in worship of Jesus and in service to man. So, Bob, too, was right. But as we empathize, we suffer and we begin to sacrifice. The question Anselm's detractors threw at him: "What kind of love demands the sacrifice of his own son in order to forgive those, for whom forgiveness has already been decreed," is the wrong question. Such a question reveals how trivial we have become. A more proper question would be, "To what extent can that, which does not demand sacrifice, be considered to be love?" It is a surprising question but then:

God is love, and all God does is just. God is not willing that any should perish nor does he delight in the death of sinners. It is through sin that death came into the world, and yet all things are possible with God. Could we not have been created to live sinless lives from the beginning? Are we not promised such lives in the restored world? Yet, we were not so created and we fail. The point is that we should seek God, not with our hands laden with the fruits we have cultivated, the fruit we have righteously wrested from the thorny soil by the sweat of our brow. To approach God in the way is to approach him joyfully in the flush of our success, and God does not want this. Instead, God, who sees us for the marred and evil being that we are, demands that we come to him covered with the blood of our innocent victims, and with the blood of that most terrible victim of all: his own Son. In this way, we come to him with nothing but our guilt and wait to discover whether he forgives or condemns, loves or hates us. We can only ask for mercy, and we discover that we are worshipping. What a surprise. God, who is righteousness, does not want our righteousness as though he had need of something we could give him. We do not give him glory when we spread our good deeds before him, it is ourselves we glorify. We give him glory when we acknowledge him for who he is and repent, as Job repented, and worship. God told Satan, "Thou movedst me against him, to destroy him without a cause." (Job 2:3)[28] Job told his friends that God "breaketh me with a tempest, and multiplieth my wounds without cause." (Job 9:17)[29] Job's horrified friends assured Job that he was being punished for some sin, but God vindicated Job by saying to Eliphaz, "My wrath is kindled against thee, and against thy two friends: for ye have not spoken of me the thing that is right, as my servant Job hath." (Job 42:7)[30]. What God wanted was not Job's righteousness, but his love.

What I discovered during this period of drunkenness and lament was that I was beginning to love God. My confidence lay, not in my faith, not in my repentance, not in my answer, but in him. To believe is to do the work of God, and I believed. I drank, not because I did not believe, but because I did not wish to do the will of God. What was the will of God? Why, to hunger and thirst after righteousness—his righteousness. I had desired to establish my own righteousness. I had acknowledged God. I had repented before him but my confidence had remained in myself. I had been called to fasting but I had begun to feast. I had not waited upon the Lord and my strength had not been renewed. My feast had turned to ashes in my mouth. It was a supper of clay, and yet my vine had brought forth the fruit of faith and repentance. Now, God was pruning it to make it bring forth a greater fruit: the fruit of love. I thought I had put down the cross. I discovered instead that I was still burdened by it. My flesh heaved against it, for my flesh knew this cross would kill it even as it had killed the flesh of the Lord. But no man took my life from me. My life was claimed by the terrible (unconditional) love of God.

Ephesians 3:16-21

I pray that from his glorious, unlimited resources he will empower you with inner strength through his Spirit. Then Christ will make his home in your hearts as you trust in him. Your roots will grow down into God's love and keep you strong. And may you have the power to understand, as all

God's people should, how wide, how long, how high, and how deep his love is. May you experience the love of Christ, though it is too great to understand fully. Then you will be made complete with all the fullness of life and power that comes from God.

Now all glory to God, who is able, through his mighty power at work within us, to accomplish infinitely more than we might ask or think. Glory to him in the church and in Christ Jesus through all generations forever and ever! Amen.

Holy Bible, New Living Translation ®, copyright © 1996, 2004 by Tyndale Charitable Trust. Used by permission of Tyndale House Publishers. All rights reserved.

A profile of Ben Michael "Mike" Carter Ph.D.

The bare bones are that Mike was born in Dallas, Texas December 31st, 1949 to Hilda & Benny Carter. Benny Carter was drafted in 1945 and served in the Philippines and Japan with the U.S. Army. Hilda Carter was a direct descendent of John Hancock, one of the founding fathers of the United States of America. When John Hancock signed his name he wrote larger than any of the others so King George of England could read it.

Mike came to know Christ in 1978 and was baptised while living in Puerto Rico. In 1980 he met Salma Carunia in Puerto Rico at Libreria Bethania while doing her internship from Bethany Missionary College, Minneapolis, Minnesota. In 1982 he married the love of his life. Mike & Salma traveled far and wide for education and missionary purposes. Subsequently, Mike earned several university degrees. He also published five books. In 2005 Mike suffered an untimley death at the age of 55 in Irving, Texas.

The legacy he left, however, is a living tri-fold. All of his searching, questions, and aspirations are documented for others to take heart, follow, and study.

A Life in Community with Thought and Reason

Mike continually sought out the place of faith within the context of reason and the world. His path left deeply affected friends, family and many acquaintances that he met in places across the globe. As he matured and traveled, Mike confronted the typical issues of a modern young man. Yet he never retreated from duties or from offering kindness to all. However, much more than a typical person, Mike not only wrestled with his doubts and the why and how of things, but he documented this struggle in an unpublished manuscript titled

102

"The Clay Supper". Salma Carter has now prepared it for publication. Mike recorded his thoughts, questions and views in extremely well written notes, letters, stories, books, poetry, and unpublished papers.

These questions and writings, his thinking therein, corresponded and developed with the events which marked his life. His mother, Hilda Carter, had tremendous influence on his life. Hilda read books to Mike at an early age. Mike was able to read to the neighborhood children at age 3. She was stricken with polio when she was 21. Mike was two years old at the time. Hilda displayed the fortitude of her distant revolutionary relative John Hancock. In spite of confinement to a wheelchair for fifty-six years she raised Mike and his younger brother James Patrick and kept the family together.

Family Travels and Military Service

Mike's father Benny Carter worked seven days a week to support his family. The Carter family moved several times as his father transferred to different locations while working with Roadway Express. He started as a clerk and worked his way up to a district superintendent . The family lived in Dallas, Irving, and San Antonio, Texas. They moved to Alaska in July 1955. Then to North Carolina in 1959, back to Irving, on to Miami, Oklahoma, Milwaukee, Wisconsin, Chicago, Illinois, and finally back to Irving, Texas.

Mike graduated from high school while in Wisconsin in 1968. He entered the The University of Wisconsin, Milwaukee in the fall of 1968. He graduated in the spring of 1972 with a B.A in History with a minor in Economics. He then enlisted in the U.S. Army.

Mike's service in the United States Army provided the initial broader view of the world. He was stationed in the DMZ of Korea and in the Panama Canal Zone and earned the Army Forces Expeditionary Medal and a United Nations Service Badge.

After his honorable discharge, he worked for a time in Milwaukee then left to travel within the continental United States and beyond. His papers reveal he was one of the many young men in the seventies searching for meaning in the post Vietnam world. Finally, while searching for the truth, he landed at the Salvation Army in Puerto Rico where he found Christ.

Higher Education and World Travels

Mike never ceased to wonder and question. With a new wife Salma and growing sense of purpose he began to study with a new direction. He earned a M.A. in Theological Studies from Billy Graham Center, Wheaton College, Illinois, a M.Th. from the University of Aberdeen in Scotland, U.K., and a Ph.D. in History of Christianity in the Non-Western World from the University of Edinburgh in Scotland United Kingdom. These gave him the intellectual tools to challenge common place thinking.

While studying at Edinburgh University Mike, Salma worked and grew alongside her husband. Mike was proud of his wife. She stood beside **Queen Elizabeth II**, when she came to open the new Glass Theater where Salma worked. Salma also received an award from The Rank Enterprise & Innovation at Odean Theater which was signed by actor **Liam Neeson** who came for the premiere of Rob Roy. In July 1997, Salma went to Europe with Plymouth Park Methodist Church Choir and sang in Switzerland, Austria and Prague, Czech Republic.

Salma also sang at Carnegie Concert Hall in New York in 1998. Salma Carunia, who was raised in a Christian orphanage in south India (the world famous **Dohnavur Fellowship established in 1901 by Amy Carmichael**), traveled the world with her husband. While teaching in China (1989-1992), Mike & Salma traveled to India to visit Dohnavur Fellowship of Amy Carmichael, where Salma was raised. Mike was very impressed with Amy Carmicheal's work, and he considered her as one of the **greatest missionaries of the 20th century!** Mike continued to place the real flesh and burdens of the world in front of his faith.

Mike's poetry and books brought him into further contact with personalities worldwide, including those scientific authors espousing purely mechanistic beginnings to our world. From these and other situations, Mike remained faithful in his **quest** and found the **answer** for us. He continued to challenge, write, publish, and dialogue with intellectuals, scientists, and authors across the world. His life ended while working for a health care company.

An Appreciation of the World, but not in it

In addition to Mike's publications and unpublished works, he demonstrated in his poetry, stories and behavior an appreciation of the world's natural beauty; a reflection of God's light unto all. He rejected the nattering of our commercial institutions in favor of worship, achieving intellectual understanding, and the nurturing of the relationship with his beloved wife, Salma Carunia. The volume of his writings speak to his ultimate acceptance and vigorous defense of a Lutheran Doctrine and yet his voice gives a far more ecumenical view of grace and a strong affirmation of one's need to actively praise & worship with love. Mike speaks with clarity and fervor that contrasts the typical staid mainstream positions of today's

Church. Mike believed God's communication to us and our expression of love through praise and worshiping Him is the core of our calling.

Biblical References:

---

[1] *Galatians 3:28 (KJV)*

[28]There is neither Jew nor Greek, there is neither bond nor free, there is neither male nor female: for ye are all one in Christ Jesus.

[2] *Ephesians 6:1 (KJV)*

[1]Children, obey your parents in the Lord: for this is right.

[3] *Genesis 26:34-35 (KJV)*

[34]And Esau was forty years old when he took to wife Judith the daughter of Beeri the Hittite, and Bashemath the daughter of Elon the Hittite:

[35]Which were a grief of mind unto Isaac and to Rebekah.

[4] *Deuteronomy 32:35 (KJV)*

[35]To me belongeth vengeance and recompence; their foot shall slide in due time: for the day of their calamity is at hand, and the things that shall come upon them make haste.

[5] *Revelation 16:13-14 (KJV)*

[13]And I saw three unclean spirits like frogs come out of the mouth of the dragon, and out of the mouth of the beast, and out of the mouth of the false prophet.

[14]For they are the spirits of devils, working miracles, which go forth unto the kings of the

*earth and of the whole world, to gather them
to the battle of that great day of God
Almighty.*

⁶ *Matthew 12:36-37 (KJV)*

³⁶But I say unto you, That every idle word that men shall
speak, they shall give account thereof in the day of judgment.

³⁷For by thy words thou shalt be justified, and by thy words
thou shalt be condemned.

⁷ *Revelation 21:5 (KJV)*

⁵And he that sat upon the throne said, Behold, I make all
things new. And he said unto me, Write: for these words are
true and faithful.

⁸ *Luke 12:18-21(KJV)*

¹⁸And he said, This will I do: I will pull down my barns, and
build greater; and there will I bestow all my fruits and my
goods.

¹⁹And I will say to my soul, Soul, thou hast much goods laid
up for many years; take thine ease, eat, drink, and be merry.

²⁰But God said unto him, Thou fool, this night thy soul shall
be required of thee: then whose shall those things be, which
thou hast provided?

²¹So is he that layeth up treasure for himself, and is not rich

toward God.

[9] *Hebrews 6:4-6 (King James Version)*

[4]For it is impossible for those who were once enlightened, and have tasted of the heavenly gift, and were made partakers of the Holy Ghost,

[5]And have tasted the good word of God, and the powers of the world to come,

[6]If they shall fall away, to renew them again unto repentance; seeing they crucify to themselves the Son of God afresh, and put him to an open shame.

[10] *John 5:16 (KJV)*

[16]And therefore did the Jews persecute Jesus, and sought to slay him, because he had done these things on the sabbath day.

[11] *Matthew 12:31-32 (KJV)*

[31]Wherefore I say unto you, All manner of sin and blasphemy shall be forgiven unto men: but the blasphemy against the Holy Ghost shall not be forgiven unto men.

[32]And whosoever speaketh a word against the Son of man, it shall be forgiven him: but whosoever speaketh against the Holy Ghost, it shall not be forgiven him, neither in this world, neither in the world to come.

[12] *Micah 6:8 (KJV)*

[8]He hath shewed thee, O man, what is good; and what doth the

LORD require of thee, but to do justly, and to love mercy, and to walk humbly with thy God?

13 *2 Thessalonians 3:10 (KJV)*

[10]For even when we were with you, this we commanded you, that if any would not work, neither should he eat.

14 *Philippians 4:8-9 (KJV)*

[8]Finally, brethren, whatsoever things are true, whatsoever things are honest, whatsoever things are just, whatsoever things are pure, whatsoever things are lovely, whatsoever things are of good report; if there be any virtue, and if there be any praise, think on these things.

[9]Those things, which ye have both learned, and received, and heard, and seen in me, do: and the God of peace shall be with you.

15 *Romans 8:22(KJV)*

[22]For we know that the whole creation groaneth and travaileth in pain together until now.

16 *Matthew 23 (KJV)*

Matthew 23

[1]Then spake Jesus to the multitude, and to his disciples,

[2]Saying The scribes and the Pharisees sit in Moses' seat:

³All therefore whatsoever they bid you observe, that observe and do; but do not ye after their works: for they say, and do not.

⁴For they bind heavy burdens and grievous to be borne, and lay them on men's shoulders; but they themselves will not move them with one of their fingers.

⁵But all their works they do for to be seen of men: they make broad their phylacteries, and enlarge the borders of their garments,

⁶And love the uppermost rooms at feasts, and the chief seats in the synagogues,

⁷And greetings in the markets, and to be called of men, Rabbi, Rabbi.

⁸But be not ye called Rabbi: for one is your Master, even Christ; and all ye are brethren.

⁹And call no man your father upon the earth: for one is your Father, which is in heaven.

¹⁰Neither be ye called masters: for one is your Master, even Christ.

¹¹But he that is greatest among you shall be your servant.

¹²And whosoever shall exalt himself shall be abased; and he that shall humble himself shall be exalted.

¹³But woe unto you, scribes and Pharisees, hypocrites! for ye shut up the kingdom of heaven against men: for ye neither go in yourselves, neither suffer ye them that are entering to go in.

¹⁴Woe unto you, scribes and Pharisees, hypocrites! for ye devour widows' houses, and for a pretence make long prayer: therefore ye shall receive the greater damnation.

¹⁵Woe unto you, scribes and Pharisees, hypocrites! for ye compass sea and land to make one proselyte, and when he is made, ye make him twofold more the child of hell than yourselves.

¹⁶Woe unto you, ye blind guides, which say, Whosoever shall swear by the temple, it is nothing; but whosoever shall swear by the gold of the temple, he is a debtor!

¹⁷Ye fools and blind: for whether is greater, the gold, or the temple that sanctifieth the gold?

¹⁸And, Whosoever shall swear by the altar, it is nothing; but whosoever sweareth by the gift that is upon it, he is guilty.

¹⁹Ye fools and blind: for whether is greater, the gift, or the altar that sanctifieth the gift?

²⁰Whoso therefore shall swear by the altar, sweareth by it, and by all things thereon.

²¹And whoso shall swear by the temple, sweareth by it, and by him that dwelleth therein.

²²And he that shall swear by heaven, sweareth by the throne of God, and by him that sitteth thereon.

²³Woe unto you, scribes and Pharisees, hypocrites! for ye pay tithe of mint and anise and cummin, and have omitted the weightier matters of the law, judgment, mercy, and faith: these ought ye to have done, and not to leave the other undone.

²⁴Ye blind guides, which strain at a gnat, and swallow a camel.

²⁵Woe unto you, scribes and Pharisees, hypocrites! for ye

make clean the outside of the cup and of the platter, but within they are full of extortion and excess.

26Thou blind Pharisee, cleanse first that which is within the cup and platter, that the outside of them may be clean also.

27Woe unto you, scribes and Pharisees, hypocrites! for ye are like unto whited sepulchres, which indeed appear beautiful outward, but are within full of dead men's bones, and of all uncleanness.

28Even so ye also outwardly appear righteous unto men, but within ye are full of hypocrisy and iniquity.

29Woe unto you, scribes and Pharisees, hypocrites! because ye build the tombs of the prophets, and garnish the sepulchres of the righteous,

30And say, If we had been in the days of our fathers, we would not have been partakers with them in the blood of the prophets.

31Wherefore ye be witnesses unto yourselves, that ye are the children of them which killed the prophets.

32Fill ye up then the measure of your fathers.

33Ye serpents, ye generation of vipers, how can ye escape the damnation of hell?

34Wherefore, behold, I send unto you prophets, and wise men, and scribes: and some of them ye shall kill and crucify; and some of them shall ye scourge in your synagogues, and persecute them from city to city:

35That upon you may come all the righteous blood shed upon the earth, from the blood of righteous Abel unto the blood of Zacharias son of Barachias, whom ye slew between the temple and the altar.

³⁶Verily I say unto you, All these things shall come upon this generation.

³⁷O Jerusalem, Jerusalem, thou that killest the prophets, and stonest them which are sent unto thee, how often would I have gathered thy children together, even as a hen gathereth her chickens under her wings, and ye would not!

³⁸Behold, your house is left unto you desolate.

³⁹For I say unto you, Ye shall not see me henceforth, till ye shall say, Blessed is he that cometh in the name of the Lord.

¹⁷ *Matthew 12:50 (KJV)*

⁵⁰For whosoever shall do the will of my Father which is in heaven, the same is my brother, and sister, and mother.

¹⁸ *Matthew 8:11 (KJV)*

¹¹And I say unto you, That many shall come from the east and west, and shall sit down with Abraham, and Isaac, and Jacob, in the kingdom of heaven.

¹⁹ *James 1:13 (KJV)*

¹³Let no man say when he is tempted, I am tempted of God: for God cannot be tempted with evil, neither tempteth he any man.

²⁰ *Job 23:10 (KJV)*

¹⁰But he knoweth the way that I take: when he hath tried me, I shall come forth as gold.

[21] 2 Peter 1:16 (KJV

[16]For we have not followed cunningly devised fables, when we made known unto you the power and coming of our Lord Jesus Christ, but were eyewitnesses of his majesty.

2 Peter 2:3 (KJV)

[3]And through covetousness shall they with feigned words make merchandise of you: whose judgment now of a long time lingereth not, and their damnation slumbereth not.

[22] Genesis 1:1 (KJV)

[1]In the beginning God created the heavens and the earth.

[23] Matthew 5:9 (KJV)

[9]Blessed are the peacemakers: for they shall be called the children of God.

[24] Matthew 10:34 (KJV)

[34]Think not that I am come to send peace on earth: I came not to send peace, but a sword.

[25] Pr 31:31 (KJV)

31 Give her of the fruit of her hands; and let her own works praise her in the gates.

26 *2 Kings 24:8 (KJV)*

⁸Jehoiachin was eighteen years old when he began to reign, and he reigned in Jerusalem three months. And his mother's name was Nehushta, the daughter of Elnathan of Jerusalem.

27 *2 Chronicles 36:9 (KJV)*

⁹Jehoiachin was eight years old when he began to reign, and he reigned three months and ten days in Jerusalem: and he did that which was evil in the sight of the LORD.

28 *Job 2:3 (KJV)*

³And the LORD said unto Satan, Hast thou considered my servant Job, that there is none like him in the earth, a perfect and an upright man, one that feareth God, and escheweth evil? And still he holdeth fast his integrity, although thou movedst me against him, to destroy him without cause.

29 *Job 9:17 (KJV)*

¹⁷For he breaketh me with a tempest, and multiplieth my wounds without cause.

30 *Job 42:7 (KJV)*

⁷And it was so, that after the LORD had spoken these words unto Job, the LORD said to Eliphaz the Temanite, My wrath

kindled against thee, and against thy two friends: for ye have not spoken of me the thing that is right, as my servant Job hath.